CONCILIUM

THEOLOGY IN THE AGE OF RENEWAL

CONCILIUM

CONCILIUM / VOL. 13

PASTORAL THEOLOGY

RE-THINKING
THE
CHURCH'S
MISSION

Volume 13

CONCILIUM
theology in the age of renewal

PAULIST PRESS
NEW YORK, N.Y. / GLEN ROCK, N.J.

NIHIL OBSTAT: Joseph F. Donahue, S.J., S.T.D.
Censor Deputatus

IMPRIMATUR: ✠ Bernard J. Flanagan, D.D.
Bishop of Worcester

March 4, 1966

The Nihil Obstat and Imprimatur are official declarations that a book or pamphlet is free of doctrinal or moral error. No implication is contained therein that those who have granted the Nihil Obstat and Imprimatur agree with the contents, opinions or statements expressed.

Library of Congress Catalogue Card Number: 66-20894

Suggested Decimal Classification: 260

BOOK DESIGN: Claude Ponsot

Paulist Press assumes responsibility for the accuracy of the English translations in this Volume.

PAULIST PRESS
EXECUTIVE OFFICES: 304 W. 58th Street, New York, N.Y. and 21 Harristown Road, Glen Rock, N.J.
Executive Publisher: John A. Carr, C.S.P.
Executive Manager: Alvin A. Illig, C.S.P.
Asst. Executive Manager: Thomas E. Comber, C.S.P.

EDITORIAL OFFICES: 304 W. 58th Street, New York, N.Y.
Editor: Kevin A. Lynch, C.S.P.
Managing Editor: Urban P. Intondi

Printed and bound in the United States of America by
The Colonial Press Inc., Clinton, Mass.

CONTENTS

PART I

ARTICLES

Eugene Hillman, C.S.Sp./ *Tanzania, East Africa*

The Main Task of
the Mission

Almost two thousand years have gone by since Christ gave the command to preach the Good News to every nation as a witness. One might well have expected the bearers of these tidings to have come to some common understanding during all this time about the exact meaning of this task insofar as the field of activity and organization are concerned. One would have expected some certainty of purpose and direction, some clear order of priority in these apostolic labors. We have already had five encyclicals on the subject in which the aims and methods of the Church's missionary task have been set out. But, with at most a fleeting acknowledgement of these

EDITORIAL NOTE: This article by an American missionary in Africa was written at a time when the Council had not yet disposed of the *Decree on the Church's Missionary Activity*. His basic thesis that mission among non-Christian peoples and pastoral care of the Christian people (even though largely dechristianized) are two wholly different tasks of the Church has been accepted by the Decree since then. However, this does not diminish the relevance of the article, for it establishes this thesis in a theologically original fashion and is here offered for discussion. He establishes that the visible Churches are set up among *each* people as a sacramental sign of salvation for *all*. As such, the sign is valid for *all* the ages of such a people and also for those who do not belong to the Church as a visible community. Thus, it links a hopeful optimism of salvation for all (often experienced in practice as undermining the missionary will) with a determined missionary intent in an inward unity.   KARL RAHNER

writings, many Catholic authors today present the missionary activity of the Church more and more as something that concerns the cultural environment of Europe and America: they speak of a "mission to the working classes", a "mission to the agricultural population", a "mission to the intellectuals" and so on, and, in general, "a mission to the dechristianized masses" that must be won back and protected against communism. At least one member of the conciliar commission for the missions was of the opinion that "the missions of the Church were not merely a matter for Africa and Asia, but for New York, Chicago, Boston, London and Paris".[1] At least one cardinal wrote about the missions as if they almost exclusively concerned the apostasy and loss of faith among the masses of Europe: the masses there were an unlimited field for missionary activity, and this activity should be directed to "every individual without exception" and "would never end".[2] Likewise, a prominent theologian has written a "Theology of the Mission" in which he makes it the duty of every French Catholic to become a missionary in pursuit of the "lost sheep" in his own community and his own milieu, without breathing a word about the duty of this same Christian to take part in the missionary task of the whole Church, the world mission to the nations that have not yet been evangelized. Yet, these nations constitute two-thirds of humanity outside the cultural sphere of the old Christendom.[3]

With this new orientation of the Church's missionary activity, it should be possible for Christians everywhere to increase their missionary zeal that would demand no greater sacrifices than those they have always made in the cause of the Church's expansion among the peoples of the non-Western world. And so, the Church could, with a quiet conscience, remain predominantly an affair of Europe and America where already more than 90% of her visible community live. But "thorough pastoral work" among these already existing communities would without

---

[1] F. Sheen, *Worldmission 1963*, Vol. 14, n. 3, p. 12.
[2] L. Suenens, *The Gospel to Every Creature* (London, 1956).
[3] A. Henry, *A Mission Theology* (Notre Dame, 1962).

doubt make increasing demands on our missionary potential, although this is as yet no more than a drop in the ocean, a mere handful compared with the number of priests and religious that serve the Christian communities. A few foreign missionaries could, like members of a private club, carry on with the work they have been doing for so long and devote themselves to the "supererogatory works of charity" at the periphery of the "Christian world" in which the Church goes about her really serious task: to look after the *domestici fidei,* the faithful of the household, "at home".

But is this the Catholic view? Where is our "home"? Before we accept this peculiar idea, according to which our missionary activity should become inward-looking, and concentrate on the society of those countries where the Church has already been firmly established, we should ask ourselves a few questions and try to find some answers.

It is true that the Church of today has to cope in many places with urgent social and pastoral problems that demand large-scale involvement of the whole Church. But should these problems be confused with the missionary task of the whole Church? Archbishop Eugene D'Souza has already drawn the attention of the Council fathers to the fact that at the moment less than 5% of the Church's activity in the world is devoted to the evangelization of "every tribe, and tongue, and people, and nation" for whom up till now the Church has never become a "naturalized" reality.[4] Should these small resources of foreign missions now be sacrificed in order to stop the progress of a political and economic ideology, to renew the remains of an old Christendom and perhaps build an everlasting kingdom on this earth? Can one compare the "cultural environment" of Europe and America with "every tribe, and tongue, and people" of the whole world? Have we given any thought to the importance for the mission of

[4] Vatican Council II, speech during the second session on "The Missionary Task of the Church," Oct. 1963. Cf. *Council Speeches of Vatican II,* eds. H. Küng, Y. Congar and D. O'Hanlon (Glen Rock, N.J.: Paulist Press, 1964).

that natural category of men, the "gentes" (or *ethne*), so often
mentioned in Scripture, or the "ethnici" of the encyclicals on the
missions? Should what little missionary strength we have be absorbed by fields where the good seed has already been sown?

There is nothing ambiguous about the missionary purpose of
the Church. At least there has not been so far. Missionary activity has never been defensive or preventive and cannot be so
by its very nature. Since the days of St. Paul, the missionary
has never been concerned with preaching the Gospel "where
Christ has already been named",[5] but with "bringing about obedience to the faith for the sake of his name among all the nations" [6] that have not yet believed. There is no question here of
building or rebuilding on foundations that have already been
laid, nor of the conversion of every individual in any given region to the visible Church. The question has always been to lay
a foundation for the Church among new peoples.[7] The Apostle
of the Gentiles did not allow himself to be wholly absorbed by
pastoral care for the already existing Church.[8] For him, as for
the fathers of Vatican Council I, the Church is a sign of salvation to be set up among the nations as an appeal to all those who
have not yet believed.[9] "He will raise an ensign for the nations,
and will assemble the outcasts of Israel, and gather the dispersed
of Judah from the four corners of the earth." [10]

Missionary activity, therefore, must consist, first of all and
specifically, in setting up this sign among more and more peoples
who have not yet known Christ through a Church firmly established among them. The grace of salvation is within reach of *all*
men[11] since Christ acquired it "once for all" [12] for *all* men by
his death and resurrection. From the beginning till the end of
time, the Word of God enlightens "every man that comes into

[5] Rom. 15, 19-21.
[6] Rom. 1, 5.
[7] 1 Cor. 3, 10.
[8] 1 Cor. 1, 17.
[9] Denzinger-Bannwart, n. 1794.
[10] Is. 11, 10-2.
[11] John 1, 1-18.
[12] Heb. 9, 26.

the world",[13] and, without compulsion, offers the same grace of salvation to everyone living in his own transient space-and time-conditioned experience of mankind's communal history. *For many* who have not known Christ, either in prophecy or in the flesh or in his sacramental Church, *are called,* like Abel, through the righteousness of their desire which the Christian tradition has always recognized as a kind of baptism. For neither the old Israel nor the new one has the monopoly of grace. Grace remains offered to all men, wherever they are and in every period of history. *But few are chosen* from *every* people to form the *visible* Church on earth.

It is an historical fact that only a relatively small minority of redeemed human beings are chosen to constitute that "small flock" which is the visible witness of the sacramental Church that must be founded once for all in every nation in order to signify and "repeat" sacramentally what Christ has achieved once for all. This sign of salvation, which the missionary labor of the whole Church must erect little by little everywhere among all the nations, is the ensign to which the chosen witnesses of God are called "from every tribe, and tongue, and people, and nation"[14] in order to found the new Israel in every nation so that the whole world can see it.

The real task of the Church's mission is therefore to be defined as follows: "As all know, the first aim of these sacred enterprises is that the light of the Christian truth may more richly shine upon the new peoples, and that there be new Christians. It is necessary, however, to aim—as the ultimate goal to be kept constantly before our eyes—at establishing the Church among other nations on a firm basis and at providing this Church with a hierarchy of her own, chosen from among the native people." [15] When this has once been achieved in a nation, the real task of the mission is "fulfilled".[16] Therefore, the task is not one that continues indefinitely, not even till every contemporary individ-

[13] John 1, 9.
[14] Rev. 5, 9.
[15] Pius XII, *Evangelii Praecones,* A.A.S. (1951), p. 507.
[16] Benedict XV, *Maximum illud,* A.A.S. (1919), p. 445.

ual has been converted to the visible membership of the Church. It is an eschatological function of the Church, and the Church herself belongs to this irreversible and unrepeatable history of mankind, feeding herself on this accomplishment of her mission. This fulfillment takes place in the same irrevocable way as all other historical and social circumstances and events which appear only once and, in succession, unfold themselves, develop collectively and are fulfilled in the one final end that is set for every creature.

The history of Christianity does not turn round and round one section of humanity but proceeds on a single path from Alpha to Omega, who is the Lord of all.[17] Every event unfolds gradually within the continuity of a single historical organism, in that it becomes what it is; what happened before is therefore no less valid than what is and what will be; every historical moment looks forward and backward in the one total history and has significance for the whole of it. Thus, every discernible people, even though unknown to all the other peoples, contributes in its own way and progressively to the development of God's kingdom. This kingdom lives invisibly in the heart of man before and after it has become visibly recognizable in the Church as it gets historically founded in one people after another. This historical progress of redeemed mankind is *part* of the task to restore the image of God in the whole man, and the grace for this restoration is given in Christ to all, everywhere and always.

For God, there is no before and after. The first are the last and the last are the first, for mankind is called as one whole. But because of the way mankind is constituted, the Church— Christ sacramentally present in time and space—has the historical task to recapitulate all in a visible sign of unity. This sign is the Church: the kingdom which comes to all men *sacramentally,* Christ and his work made present within the tangible history of one people after another in forms expressed by all who are chosen to bear witness through an explicit faith in Christ. These forms express the universal and always actual

[17] Rev. 21, 6; Acts 10, 36.

salvation of mankind, obtained once and for all by Christ at a specific point within the history of a given ethnic and cultural group of people. Just as the Word once became flesh in the physical body of the historically chosen people, so must the Church *once* become "flesh" sacramentally in the body of any given "chosen" people by presenting actively and "sacramentally" among the peoples in time and space what Christ fulfilled once for all.

It is an intrinsic element of the missionary task of the Church to bring about these "sacramental" bodies once for all by calling the chosen witnesses, the still dispersed remnants, from among the tribes, tongues, peoples and nations that are looking for the ensign which will call them home to the new Israel. The missionary task, which consists in setting up the ensign of salvation once for all for every nation, can be accomplished and can be repeated. It consists in a successive achievement of the aim to bring about, in one people after another, the progressive preparation for the final advent of the Lord at the end of this world and to establish the sign itself of this advent. Like the Church herself, this task is a sacramental sign of the coming of the Lord in glory, when "every eye will see him . . . and all tribes of the earth will wail on account of him".[18] It is a sign of hope for all who love his coming and the measure of their desire for his presence. "And the Gospel must first be preached to all nations" . . . "as a testimony to all nations, and then the end will come." [19] The fulfillment of the Church's missionary task as the necessary sign of the end depends on the tangible result of the preaching of the Gospel. It is not a matter of the total conversion of every individual in every place to the visible Church: only a few are chosen for this. Nor does the completion of this task depend on the historical endurance of the visible Church among a given people: she is not meant to be an eternal kingdom anywhere on earth. Even during the last days, after the Gospel has been preached everywhere, many will fall away; and because

[18] Rev. 1, 7.
[19] Mark 13, 10; Matt. 24, 14.

wickedness is multiplied, many will be led astray and most men's love will grow cold.[20] The missionary sign of the end is achieved simply when the Gospel has been preached to all peoples, when the "door of faith" has been opened to all nations,[21] when a solid foundation has been laid for the visible Church once for all in every nation. Thus, Paul was compelled to do all he could wherever possible in order "to hasten the coming of the day of God",[22] preaching to ever new nations and entrusting the young immature Christian communities to the care of their own pastors "in order to proclaim the Word fully, that all the Gentiles might hear it".[23] For every nation, as for all the world, there is the moment when the missionary task is fulfilled and has come to an end.[24]

Among all peoples the Church shares and signifies the once-for-all character of the redeeming work of Christ, which is accomplished within a history made up of transient events, and these events will only be seen in their true significance at the end. As it happens in the physical life of each man and in the historical experience of the various ethnical and cultural groups, so it is with the life of the Church: what is, what has been and what is still coming—all have an always present validity and finality in the rise and fall of growth. Nothing is repeated. When the Church has once been firmly set up among a people, her missionary task there is over. Once the good seed has been sown in a field, this field must be left to the care of the farmer till the end.[25] Missionaries must pass on to other fields where the good seed has not yet been sown. There is nothing in the Gospel about "re-evangelization". The end must come sometime. As Augustine said: "The bridegroom is absent; examine your conscience: do you want him to come, or do you want him to wait a little longer?"[26]

[20] Matt. 24, 10-26.
[21] Acts 14, 24.
[22] 2 Pet. 3, 12.
[23] 2 Tim. 4, 17.
[24] Acts 12, 25; 14, 25.
[25] Matt. 13, 24-30; 36-43.
[26] *Enarratio in Ps. 127,* 8-9 (*P.L.* 37, cc. 1681-2).

Karl Müller, S.V.D. / *Rome, Italy*

The Main Principles of Centralized Government for the Missions

" **A**mong the innumerable deeds and documents of the papal archives," wrote Prof. Mulders[1] with reference to the Protestant scholar, T. Trede,[2] "there is hardly one that is still so influential today as the Constitution *Inscrutabili Divinae Providentiae* (June 22, 1622), by which the *Propaganda Fide* (Sacred Congregation for Propagating the Faith) was finally set up." However forcefully the Roman congregations were criticized and however much one liked to talk of an *aggiornamento* of the supreme missionary authority, the basic tone of the discussions on the *Propaganda Fide* was, even in the aula of the Council, one of great respect for its achievement in the past and of a conviction that it would still play an important role in the future.

The history of Christ's incarnation in the non-Christian world, in other words, the history of the missions, is clear evidence of the divine element in the Church. The penetration into the Roman-Hellenistic world, the triumphal progress through the regions inhabited by Teutons and Slavs, the worldwide mission that began at the start of the modern age—all this is an achieve-

---

[1] A. Mulders, *Missiegeschiedenis* (Bussum, Holland, 1957); German Tr.: *Missionsgeschichte* (Regensburg, 1960), p. 259.

[2] Cf. T. Trede, *Die Propaganda Fide in Rom. Ihre Geschichte und ihre Bedeutung* (Berlin, 1884).

11

ment that goes beyond a purely natural explanation. It also shows that Christ's incarnation always takes place in a human body; that there is a human element within the mystical body of Christ, the Church; that the missionary Church must constantly struggle against what is too human in her, against purely human methods and practices, against getting entangled in purely temporal considerations and aims; and that to try to be a bride without blemish and without wrinkle is her enduring task.

I

PRIORITY OF THE RELIGIOUS AIM

The social character of man implies that the Church does not only address herself to individual human beings but can and must also address herself to human communities and to the kind of State in which they find themselves. This was the case in the empire of Constantine and among the Germanic tribes, reaching an historical climax when Pope Alexander VI drew the colonial demarcation line for Spain and Portugal with the commission: "Moreover, we charge you in virtue of holy obedience . . . to send righteous, God-fearing, wise and reliable men to these islands and this continent, who are able to guide the natives toward good moral behavior and to instruct them in the Catholic faith." [3] The right of patronage, which Spain and Portugal herewith legally obtained, was interpreted and extended by later papal Bulls. Spain and Portugal have done much in this mission field. But at the same time this gesture saddled the missions for centuries with the need to explain things and it has cast a shadow that has prolonged itself into very recent times.

The Constitution establishing the *Propaganda Fide,* mentioned at the beginning of this article, is a purely positive document and in no sense polemical. It shows that the pope was very worried about how to bring souls into the Church of Christ,[4] and hoped to draw more attention to this problem, to give it more direction

[3] Bull *Inter cetera* (Bull. Rom. V, ed. Taurin., pp. 361ff.).
[4] "Opus adductionis animarum ad Ecclesiam Christi."

and importance, by setting up a cardinalatial congregation.[5] The religious aim of the congregation is expressed in its name: it is to concern itself with the propagation of the faith and with nothing else.

Compared with this founding Bull, the *Propaganda Fide's* famous Instruction *Ad Exteros*[6] to the apostolic vicars in 1659 is wholly conditioned by contemporary history. "What is more absurd than to introduce France, Spain, Italy or any other European country into China? This is not what you should take there, but the faith!" "Teach those people to obey their authorities. . . . Do not bring any political intrigue into those regions, whether Spanish, French, Turkish, Persian or others; on the contrary, as far as you can, stamp it out radically. And if, in spite of warnings, one of your missionaries does not leave such things alone, send him back to Europe at once before his rashness endangers the very important enterprises of the Christian religion." "Since human nature is such that it esteems and loves its own, and particularly one's own people, above everything else, there is no stronger ground for hatred and antipathy than to have to change the customs of one's mother country, particularly if one's ancestors have lived there since the beginning, and this will appear true particularly when, after having done away with existing customs, one tries to impose those of one's own people." People should see in the behavior of the missionaries that they are "concerned only with what is spiritual and the salvation of souls", and that all their "work, labors and thoughts are bent only on what is heavenly, to the exclusion of everything else".

One is impressed when reading Beckmann's comprehensive article on the *Propaganda Fide* in the field of international political tensions.[7] It shows the dramatic exchanges between the congregation and the powers that were in possession of patronage

---

[5] *Collectanea S. Congregationis de Propaganda Fide* I (Rome, 1907), n. 3, pp. 2-4.

[6] *Ibid.*, I, n. 135, pp. 42f.

[7] J. Beckmann, "La Congrégation de la Propagande de la Foi face à la politique internationale," in *N. Zeitschrift Missionsw.* 19 (1963), pp. 241-71.

or protectorate, with their victories and setbacks, their stubbornness and their readiness to compromise. It was not until the 19th and (partly) 20th centuries that it succeeded in freeing the mission, at least in principle, from dependence on the secular State. For India the Concordat of 1857 and the setting up of a hierarchy by Leo XIII in 1886 were decisive, although the Brief *Multa praeclare* of Gregory XVI (1838) had led to the "schism of Goa". The same Gregory XVI began with the reorganization of Chinese territory where a new form of dependence had appeared, that of the French "protectorate", which created difficulties. In Korea an "apostolic vicariate", *i.e.,* an ecclesiastical district independent of the prevailing secular power, was already set up in 1831, though not without difficulty, since Korea belonged ecclesiastically to the diocese of Peking. In the overseas possessions of Spain the direct influence of the *Propaganda Fide* remained more or less nil until the 20th century.

Latin America had its first "apostolic vicariate" in 1874. In the Philippines the situation lasted until the apostolic vicariate of Palawan was set up in 1910. To these were added the apostolic prefectures of Montanosa and Mindoro before World War II, and that of Sulu after this same war. All three are today apostolic vicariates.

In Africa and Oceania the *Propaganda Fide* extended its influence more smoothly inasmuch as the missionary congregations, which sprang up in the 19th century, and the restored Jesuits put themselves unhesitatingly and completely at its disposal. That the *Propaganda Fide,* by using missionaries of the respective colonizing powers in the 19th century, did not identify itself with the aims, let alone the methods, of the colonizers needs hardly be mentioned.

After World War I, when there was an eruption of uncontrolled nationalism, no less a person than Benedict XV warned the missionaries: "The mission entrusted to you is plainly divine and is high above the misery of human ends. . . . Understand then that the Lord has said to each of you: 'Forget your people and your home', and remember that it is not your business to extend a human kingdom but the kingdom of Christ, that it is not your business to enlist citizens for your mother country on this earth, but for the fatherland which is above." And he had these hard words about nationalistic tendencies: "These would be a horrifying plague for apostolic labor, which would paralyze all the vigor of love for souls in the preacher of the Good News and would undermine his prestige among the people." [8]

Without going further into these statements I want to refer to the words of Pius XII who formulated the devotion and self-renouncement of the missionary in the following radical terms: "He (the missionary) must therefore look on any region where he wants to spread the light of the Gospel as his second fatherland and love it with the affection this demands. Let him not look for material advantages, nor pursue the interests of his nation or his order, but rather the salvation of souls. He will no doubt have a profound love for his nation and the members of his congregation, but he will love the Church with a far more burning zeal." [9] When we look at the "emigration" and "immigration" of the missionary with the depth of understanding demanded here, we can also understand the opinion of the Council fathers that a missionary may well be valuable for the mission, yet not correspond to the ideal the Church has of him: missionary vocation means the total giving of oneself, and this for life, to forget one's people and one's home.[10]

II

BASIC PRINCIPLE OF THE GENERAL MISSIONARY GOVERNMENT IN ROME

1. *The Priority of the Direct Apostolate*

The use of the word "priority" for the direct apostolate does not imply here anything against the importance of what is called

[8] Encyclical *Maximum illud,* Nov. 30, 1919: *A.A.S.* 11 (1919), p. 446.
[9] Encyclical *Evangelii praecones,* June 2, 1951: *A.A.S.* 43 (1951), p. 506.
[10] Cf. *Decree on the Church's Missionary Activity* of Vatican Council II, n. 24.

"pre-evangelization", which is given increased attention today and which constitutes a vital problem of missionary method. It has still less to do with that "presence of love" which has been emphasized by the Council and which is much more than a question of missionary method insofar as it is the radiating witness of a Christian existence. Whoever calls on God as Father cannot but see his brother in his fellowman, and, indeed, in every fellowman.

The use of the expression mentioned above *does,* however, imply a distinction from what is typically called "cultural mission" and also from what here and there has been observed as a kind of absolutization of the so-called "works" of charity. Charity, yes, and charity above everything else, but the "works" of charity are meant to be a service. The Synod of Juthia (1665) no doubt interpreted Christ and his message too one-sidedly when it rejected the teaching of astronomy, mathematics, painting and technical skills as "the product of a restless and ambitious soul" on the grounds that "we do not read that Christ and his apostles used such means".

Pius XII was a prominent advocate of what are called the indirect missionary means: school, press, medical care, social work. "Since one day the younger generation, particularly those with a scientific formation, higher studies, or achievements in the liberal arts, will no doubt shape the course of future eras and of history, anyone can see how important elementary and secondary schools and colleges are. . . . No less useful are the publication and distribution of timely and opportune writings. . . . And here we would recommend urgently those works and enterprises which, as far as possible, deal with illness, defectiveness and other needs. . . . We now turn to another point, not less important and not less serious. We would like to touch on some points that may lead to a solution of the social problem according to the norms of justice and love." [11]

John XXIII expressed himself more cautiously when, with

---

[11] Cf. the Encyclical *Evangelii praecones,* June 2, 1951: *A.A.S.* 43, (1951), pp. 514-7.

reference to the formation of lay helpers, he recommended the school but added: "Yet, as it is obviously difficult to integrate the formation of Catholic Action leaders into the school program, promising young people should frequently be brought together outside the school in order to be introduced and guided into the apostolate both in theory and in practice. . . . It will always remain necessary to complete the academic and vocational education they have received in the State schools with an intelligent and carefully organized spiritual formation so that people do not leave these schools wrongly instructed and puffed up with arrogance and so do more harm than good to the Church and her people. Their religious training should follow their spiritual development." [12]

The *Decree on the Church's Missionary Activity* of Vatican Council II has no chapter on schools, but in a very general way it exhorts Christians to concern themselves with, and to collaborate in "rightly regulating the affairs of social and economic life . . . let them devote themselves to the education of children and young people by means of different schools" (n. 12). Elsewhere (n. 15) the school is recommended as a means for the formation of the Christian community. But in all this one is aware here, too, of a certain reserve. The moderation maintained by the Decree may be inspired by the change in the cultural situation of the world. While in the course of history the Church was the only body that provided culture, or when the public bodies provided only a purely secular education, the Church had perforce to assume these tasks; it is a requirement of natural law and lies in the perspective of the Church's Christian mandate.[13] But the Church would prefer that other bodies take over this

[12] The Encyclical *Princeps Pastorum,* Nov. 28, 1959: *A.A.S.* 51 (1959), p. 858.

[13] It is in this sense that we may understand the addition put into the schema after the public discussion in the Council: "The faithful must devote special care to the education of children and adolescents in different types of schools. This work is to be considered not only as an excellent means for the formation and development of Christian youth, but is, at the same time, of great service to mankind, especially in the developing countries, in order to increase the sense of human dignity and to pave the way for more human living conditions" (n. 12).

work in the same spirit since it deprives her of so much strength and so many resources. Then she could concentrate wholly on her proper function, which is the preaching of God's Word.

2. *The Foundation of Episcopal Churches*

Almost at the same time as the foundation (1622) of the *Propaganda Fide,* there appeared in Spain a missionary study.[14] It proposed the interesting thesis that the proper and first missionaries should be bishops. According to the author, they were given, as successors of the apostles, the direct mission to serve as heralds; every new Church was founded in the blood of its bishop; missions in his time (the author refers principally to Japan) failed because they were led by simple priests instead of bishops as missionaries. One may wonder whether even today the bishop's function is not seen in a false light insofar as it is mainly seen as government and administration instead of preaching and the divine office. But, in any case, the author's complaint was more than justified for his days.

At the beginning of the 17th century the whole southern and eastern coast of Asia, including the islands, had only two archdioceses, Goa and Cranganor, and five dioceses, Cochin, Meliapur, Malacca, Macao and Funay. Obviously, with such vast territories under their jurisdiction, bishops had no contact with the people and the missionaries. It is equally clear that under these circumstances there was neither planning nor direction, let alone the *diaconia verbi,* the service of the Word; disorders in the apostolate could not definitely be put down and therefore could spread without control; there was no authoritative body to deal with conflicts among the missionaries; practically nothing was done to cope with the pressing need for priests and many other problems.

The *Propaganda Fide,* founded in 1622, realized very quickly that it was absolutely necessary to erect new dioceses and ap-

[14] M. Sarmiento de Mendoza, *Milicia evangelica para contrastar la idolatria de los Gentiles, conquistar almas, derribar la humana prudencia, destarrar la auaricia de ministros* (Madrid, 1628).

point bishops independent of Portugal. But this was precisely very difficult in view of the political situation inside and outside the Church.

A first measure in this direction was the appointment of an archbishop and a bishop for Japan, which belonged to the diocese of Funay, vacant for several years. Unfortunately, neither Archbishop Antonio della Madre de Dios nor Bishop Matthew de Castro reached their destination. The latter, an Indian, was nominated "administrator or vicar apostolic" of Idalcan (part of the diocese of Goa). With this appointment, a new title appears in history, namely, that of "vicar apostolic". A vicar apostolic has no ordinary jurisdiction but acts rather as the vicar of the pope. In this manner Rome hoped to bypass Portugal's right of patronage. After Idalcan they thought of also appointing vicars apostolic in Bengal, on the islands of Solor, in Macassar, Siam, Mozambique, Ceylon and other places in 1648, but difficulties with Portugal prevented this. It was not until 1659/60 that further vicars apostolic were appointed. These were the well-known Pallu, de la Motte and Cotolendi for Tonkin, Conchinchina and Nanking. Their fateful reception in the Far East is sufficiently known.

How unfortunate this dependence on non-ecclesiastical powers was can be seen, *e.g.,* in the fact that the See of Macao, which stretched over the whole of China, was vacant from 1615 until 1692. The same happened in other dioceses under the influence of the patronage system. It is therefore not astonishing that at last, in 1660, a vicar apostolic was appointed for Nanking. However, Alexander VIII allowed himself to be persuaded again to elevate Nanking and Peking into patronage dioceses. His successor, Innocent XII, tried to diminish the effect of this weakening attitude by setting up vicariates apostolic in Fukien, Szechwan and Shansi side by side with the patronage dioceses of Macao, Nanking and Peking. This arrangement lasted until the 19th century.

It would lead us too far afield to pursue the varied history of all this in detail. Today practically the whole world is divided into episcopal Churches—either member Churches or particular Churches, as they are called today. From the point of view of organization this is an impressive achievement, while theologically it means that today everywhere "sacrifice is made to his name and a spotless sacrificial bread is offered".

Joseph Ratzinger points out in a commentary on the *Constitution on the Church* that the basic shape of the Church is "the liturgical assembly", that her basic substance is "the liturgical service, the adoration of the Father through Christ in the Holy Spirit", and that the division into local Churches, *i.e.*, into a "system of liturgical communities", with "the See of Peter in Rome as the basic point of orientation which binds them together", is essential to the Church founded by Christ.[15] In this view the missionary work of the Church has made important progress since Rome again assumed direction by the foundation of the *Propaganda Fide*. This is not only true of the administrative, organizational and strategic aspect, but also, and above all, from the theological point of view. "The bishop, marked with the fullness of the sacrament of orders, is 'the steward of the grace of the supreme priesthood', especially in the eucharist, which he offers or causes to be offered, and by which the Church continually lives and grows. This Church of Christ is truly present in all legitimate local congregations of the faithful which, united with their pastors, are themselves called Churches in the New Testament. For in their own locality these are the new People called by God in the Holy Spirit and in much fullness." [16]

3. *Native Clergy and Hierarchy*

From the start the *Propaganda Fide* intended to attract priests and bishops from the missionary peoples themselves. As early as 1626 a Japanese bishop was presented with such a request.[17] Four years later a similar strongly formulated Instruction was sent to India with a reference to the example of the apostles and

[15] *Dogmatische Konstitution über die Kirche* (Münster), pp. 10 and 14.
[16] Cf. *Constitution on the Church* with commentary by Gregory Baum (Glen Rock, N.J.: Paulist Press, 1964), n. 26.
[17] Cf. *Collectanea* I, n. 1002, p. 543.

the early Church and to the greater confidence and the better knowledge of language, customs and tendencies which the native priest enjoyed.[18] The first vicars apostolic of the missionary seminary in Paris were told explicitly that "they should take care in every way and with every argument to educate the youth in such a way that they will become fit for the priesthood and be ordained".[19] The *Propaganda Fide's* Instruction of Nov. 23, 1845, alone enumerates fifteen documents in which Rome recommended the creation of an indigenous clergy. They included Innocent XI's strong threat to "force" the vicars apostolic, by means of canonical penalties, to prepare Christians from the respective countries and peoples for the priesthood and to ordain them. What was the result? Twenty-five years after the missionary seminary had been established in Paris, Tonkin had eleven and Cochinchina two indigenous priests. The first Chinese priest, Fray Gregorio Lopez, a Dominican, was ordained in 1654; in 1674 he was appointed vicar apostolic for the northern provinces of China, but, precisely because he was Chinese, he could not be consecrated bishop until 1685. Both the Indian vicars apostolic, Matthew de Castro and Custodius Pinho, were trained at the College of the Propaganda in Rome. Indeed, much happened, and yet the above-mentioned Instruction of 1845 had to state: "Sad experience shows that all the labor spent without interruption on all this has not met with the result the Apostolic See expected." [20]

Opposition to a powerful increase of indigenous clergy came, above all, from the missionaries in the field and lasted until very recently. Rome, however, consistently pursued its way. In his Encyclical *Maximum illud,* Benedict XV upheld the training of an indigenous clergy as the "main preoccupation" of the bishops and demanded a preparation "that would enable them to take over the direction of the divine service and consequently one day the direction of their own people".[21]

[18] *Ibid.*, n. 62, p. 15.
[19] *Ibid.*, n. 1002, p. 543.
[20] *Ibid.*
[21] Cf. *A.A.S.* 11 (1919), p. 445.

Cardinal van Rossum exhorted the superiors of religious orders in the following terms: "It is of the utmost importance that the superiors of the missions entrusted to their congregations should give every attention to the training of an indigenous clergy. This is indeed necessary because the various territories have been entrusted to them with the view of founding and building up the Church there. The conversion of non-believers is but the start, the first stone of this building; the formation of the Christian community must follow, with its own chapels or churches, with the foundation (and possibly the endowment) of schools, orphanages, asylums, hospitals and other works. This, however, must be followed, or rather accompanied, by the training of an indigenous clergy and indigenous religious communities of both sexes." [22] One has the impression that the members of the Commission for the Missions had this program before them when they drafted the schema on missionary activity, *De Communitate Christiana Efformanda.*

The real and irresistible breakthrough came with the pontificate of Pius XI. Apart from the energy displayed in speech and in writing, he himself ordained in 1926 the first six Chinese bishops and in 1927 the first Japanese bishop. In China the number of indigenous priests rose from 938 in 1923 to 2,022 in 1939. In India and Ceylon the number of native priests rose between 1923 and 1948 to about 2,000 while foreign priests only amounted to 761. In 1923 Indochina had 33 native priests in all, which number had increased to 82 by 1948. The first Indonesian priest was ordained at Maastricht in 1926; in 1948 there were 66.

At the end of World War I Africa had 145 native priests, 358 in 1939 and 958 in 1948, not counting Egyptian, Abyssinian and Galla priests.[23] As the number of native clergy grew, whole

---

[22] *Sylloge praecipuorum documentorum recentium Summorum Pontificum et S. Congregationis de Propaganda Fide* (Rome, 1939), n. 112, p. 215.

[23] Present figures of the native clergy are: Japan 607, South Korea 346, Formosa 298, Hongkong 107, Philippines 2316, South Vietnam 1306, Indonesia 220, India 6520; Africa has 75 African bishops (2 cardinals,

dioceses could be handed over to them, and thus more Japanese, Chinese, Filipinos, Indonesians, Indians and Africans could be made bishops, archbishops and even cardinals.

A look at the conciliar assembly shows an inspiring picture of the one Church made up of many Churches from all peoples, tribes and nations. "The Word of God is like a seed that draws vital juice from a good soil drenched with divine dew, transforms it and assimilates it. And so the seed grows and bears abundant fruit. Thus the young Churches, rooted in Christ on the foundation of the apostles, assume, through a kind of incarnation, all the riches of the nations that are Christ's heritage, in a wondrous exchange. From the customs and traditions, the wisdom and teaching, the arts and sciences of their people, these Churches borrow all that can contribute to the praise of God's glory, show forth the grace of the Savior and create a right order for Christian life" (*Decree on the Church's Missionary Activity*, n. 22).

4. *Adaptation and Incorporation*

During the last decades there has been much talk about adaptation, understood almost exclusively in the sense of a didactic and educational adaptation and hardly ever in the sense of what one might call "incorporating adaptation". Didactic and educational adaptation is necessary, but it is not a problem peculiar to the mission. A father must adapt himself to his child if he wants to transmit his own knowledge to him, and so the teacher must adapt himself to the pupil, and the parish priest to the parish child. In this sense adaptation is a universal human problem that demands not only intelligence but also love.

Oddly enough, Pius XII had a preference for terms connected with natural growth when he spoke about missionary adaptation. Thus he used to say that it would not do to uproot the "tree" of pagan culture and to "transplant" European culture in the mission countries. The missionary should rather be a clever gardener who does not destroy the "luxuriant forest", but "grafts"

---

17 archbishops, 41 bishops, 15 titular bishops) and in the regions under the Propaganda about 2500 African priests.

the true Christian "scion" on the "wild growth" [24] in order that a "new and God-willed creature" might develop from a new marriage of nature and grace, the continuation of the incarnation in a new people.

Similar imagery is found in the above-quoted text from the conciliar Decree. It speaks of "seed", of "sap" drawn from the soil, of "transformation" and "assimilation", of "growing" and the "bearing of fruit"; it uses the comparison with the "incarnation" through which human nature and divine nature unite in the unity of the person.

Here I refer again to Ratzinger's commentary on the *Constitution on the Church*. He explains that the Church as the People of God must always be a Church "on the way", and adds: "This implies that she can never rest on her laurels as if the aim had been achieved; that she must always be ready to disentangle herself from the historical roots of a given period or culture; that she must be ready to serve a new age to which she must proclaim the Word of God which remains eternal but can only live in this world by offering flesh and blood to every generation, through new experience and new suffering. This insight is decisive for the theology of the mission of which one hears the overtones in the chapter on the People of God." And he continues: "Patristic theology provides a picture with a much deeper appeal which in fact lies behind the explanations of the Constitution: the *assumptio hominis,* the assumption of man in all his historical dimensions, inaugurated in principle in the incarnation of the Word at Bethlehem. This assumption must be continued in the mission in such a way that the flesh of humanity, *i.e.,* its earthly historical existence, becomes truly the flesh of the Word, a process that cannot come about without a painful change, according to the law of the seed that cannot promise life except through the death of the self, but then can truly bear abundant fruit." [25] A superficial reading will miss a chapter on

[24] Above all in the address of 1944 to the leaders of the papal missionary societies, and in the Encyclical *Evangelii praecones.*
[25] *Op. cit.,* p. 11, footnote 15.

adaptation in the new *Decree on the Church's Missionary Activity*, but a deeper understanding will show that the whole Decree is permeated by what one can theologically designate as adaptation.

Christ, the incarnate Word of God, is sent into the world, as "the true mediator between God and men" and is, according to his human nature, "the new Adam, the head of restored humanity" (n. 3). In the execution of his mandate the whole Church cooperates, each according to his place, function and God-given vocation in the body (n. 5). The mission of the Church is nothing else but the continuation of the mission of Christ (*ibid.*). Christ, however, was sent in order to build up "one People of God", "one body of Christ", one temple of the Holy Spirit out of the multiplicity of mankind (n. 7). The formation of the Christian community among the people of the mission is seen as "the gathering into one People of God a chosen race, a royal priesthood, a holy nation, God's own people" (n. 15).

To the theological view of the total Church as "one People of God" corresponds the theological view (not the juridical and administrative one) of the local Churches: these local Churches should have their own character, their own outlook, their own importance; they must be the "People of God" as formed out of the "flesh" of the people they belong to. And so, the multiplicity of the Churches shows the richness of true unity (cf. nn. 19f.). A genuine theology of local Churches is precisely what is meant by "incorporating adaptation": all that is divine in all that is human, and vice versa; a mystical marriage between divinity and humanity that leads to a new incarnation of the Word in a new people; an "assumption of man" in a new "historical dimension". "From the beginning until our own day the Church has maintained the supremely wise rule that acceptance of the Gospel should in no way destroy or eliminate whatever is good, noble and beautiful in the nature and gifts of the various peoples. Since the Church calls the various peoples under the protection of the Christian faith to a higher way of life and to an improved way of life, she does not act like one that destroys and roots out the luxuriant forest, but rather like one that grafts a good scion onto a wild growth so that it may reach maturity and bring forth better and sweeter fruit." [26]

In what we have seen so far, it has been possible again and again to point to considerable advances in missionary enterprise. However, it must also be pointed out here that in the Latin Church we are still wholly at the beginning of the road. Our philosophy is Western, our theology is Western, our prayers and prayer gestures are Western, our liturgy is Western and the native priests and bishops are Western educated and think and feel more or less in the Western way. The breakthrough to a genuine native art and architecture is still in the future. And yet, all peoples are called to bring their own gifts to the Christmas crib. There must be multiplicity in unity. Adaptation in this sense comes very close to meaning the same thing as missionary work, at least in its final consequences. That is why the *Decree on the Church's Missionary Activity* was fully entitled not to have a special chapter on adaptation.

III

"AGGIORNAMENTO" ON THE HIGHEST LEVEL OF MISSIONARY GOVERNMENT

1. For more than a century the popes have shown a wholly personal interest in the work of the missions. Pope Gregory XVI, who was himself head of the *Propaganda Fide*, was able to go his own way without hesitation because he knew the needs of the missions like no one else. Pius XI called himself the "pope of the missions" and used every opportunity to stress the urgency of the missions and to back their affairs and progress with his full support. The personal commitment of the present pope (Paul VI) went so far that it earned him the title of "missionary". One should not look on this as some pious frivolity or as an excess prompted by reverence for the pope as head of the Church, but

[26] Pius XII, Encyclical *Evangelii praecones, op. cit.,* footnote 9.

rather as simply a concrete expression of Catholic theology. If the superior general of the missionaries of Steyl was right in saying at a recent press conference that the Church's missionary activity "is not some peripheral activity, or some voluntary hobby of some eccentric missionaries or societies, but belongs to the very essence of the Church" and that "the Council was rightly expected to bring the missions back into the very heart of the Church", then it is obvious that the pope must not have a merely general interest in the missions but it must be his personal concern. And if it is true of all the bishops that they are not merely consecrated for their dioceses but "for the salvation of the whole world", how much more does this apply to the pope who, as vicar of Christ on earth, has as his main task to promote the incarnation of Christ in all peoples.

2. In his Motu Proprio, *Apostolica Sollicitudo*, September 15, 1965,[27] the pope laid down that the change in the demands of the age and the development of human society required other methods. He speaks of "signs of the time" and sees himself compelled to work in closer and stronger union with the episcopate in the "government of the Church" (Acts 20, 28). In this he was not prompted by respect for the bishops, but it was imposed on him by "the most heavy burden of the universal pastor" that had been put on his shoulders. "The present age, full of unrest and distress, but also open to the sanctifying inspiration of divine grace, makes us feel daily how much our apostolic office is helped by this collaboration with the consecrated pastors, so that we wish to promote and use it in every way." For that purpose he instituted a "standing conference of bishops" to which he gave the name of "episcopal synod".

According to the Motu Proprio this episcopal synod has an advisory function; there is no mention of a share in the government, apart from the quotation from the Acts. The *Decree on the Church's Missionary Activity* goes a step further in the interpretation of the principle of collegiality, on the basis of the *Constitution on the Church*: the care for the preaching of the

[27] Cf. *L'Osservatore Romano,* Sept. 26, 1965.

Gospel throughout the world is "the business of the body of bishops", and so "among the duties of a more general kind, the question of the missions deserves particular attention in the central council of the Pope as the most holy and the most important task of the Church" (n. 29). Whatever interpretation one may give to this episcopal synod, the members of this "central council" of the pope are thought of as representing the body of bishops, and as such they must be particularly concerned with the missionary activity of the Church in principle, and not merely as a positive task, precisely because they represent the body of bishops.

The institution of the episcopal synod may have very fruitful results for the missionary work of the Church, and this in the same way in which the Council itself had a fruitful influence on the missions of the world. As Fr. Johannes Schütte, S.V.D., said at the press conference mentioned above: "It is at a Council that the world mission plays a decisive part through its many-sided and constantly observable presence." In the future this presence of the world mission will be permanently felt in the Church through its representatives in the episcopal synod. The episcopal conferences of Japan, Indonesia, India and Africa will send their representatives to the synod as much as those of the United States, Spain, France or Poland—one, two, three or even four— according to the membership of the episcopal conferences. The missionary orders, too, who still bear the brunt of the daily missionary labor, will be represented by a number of superiors general, as laid down in the Motu Proprio. In the future the mission will have its say in the government of the Church, will present its problems and worries and will be a constant reminder to the bishops of the already established Churches. By meeting the problems in its own way it will encourage, inspire and console the bishops of the mother countries. The mission will add its own peculiar riches to the whole Church so that her beauty and light will be enhanced and her message more enlightening and convincing. On the other hand, the Churches of the mother countries will become more humble, more ready for service and the practice of the Gospel, more ready to provide all possible assistance for the brothers and sisters far away in their material and spiritual needs, and more ready to put their experience at the service of the younger Churches that still look for ways of solving their difficulties.

3. The *sacrum commercium,* the sacred exchange, which is so essential in the new view of the Church, will be permanently stimulated through the powerful symbol of the episcopal synod. From what has been already said about the *Propaganda Fide* as the competent authority for the missions, it is clear that it did not only possess sound principles but that it applied these principles rightly or wrongly as far as circumstances allowed. The Protestant missionary scholar, G. Warneck, called the *Propaganda Fide* "one of the greatest institutions of the world", and the historian, L. von Ranke, said: "The *Propaganda* nobly tried to fulfill its task, and perhaps most nobly at the beginning." The historical merit of the *Propaganda Fide* and its methods of dealing with the representatives of the missions were fully admitted by the Council fathers, as has already been observed.

If there was, nevertheless, talk of an *aggiornamento* of this well-deserving congregation, it arose from the principle, laid down by John XXIII in his Encyclical *Mater et Magistra,* that today any problem of some significance, whether it be scientific, technical, economic, social, political or cultural, surpassed the capacity of a single institution and could only be solved in an international and worldwide context.[28] And although this principle is a proof for the justification, and indeed the necessity, of a central authority for the missions, it recommends and even demands a structural adaptation to the modern age.

The *Decree on the Church's Missionary Activity* imposes upon the *Propaganda Fide* an almost impossible task of administration: it includes the "direction and coordination" of the whole mission and the missionary labor itself, as well as the help provided by the mother countries. According to its view, the *Propaganda Fide* must concern itself with the vocation and proper

[28] *A.A.S.* 53 (1961), p. 449.

spirituality of the missionaries, urge missionary zeal, recommend prayer for the mission and provide information about the mission; it must find missionaries and use them according to the need of the missions; it must plan missionary operation, formulate its norms and directives and provide it with the necessary stimulus; it must raise the level of material assistance, distributing it with care and according to a plan, giving due consideration to urgency, usefulness, the expansion of missionary territories, the relative proportion of believers and non-believers, charities and institutions, helpers and missionaries. In view of such tasks the administration and direction of this authoritative body must show some dynamism, use scientific methods and modern means, and not forget to exploit the results of modern theological, methodological and pastoral thought. In order to do justice to all this, two new concrete propositions have been made:

(a) The congregation must be composed of representatives of all those who collaborate in missionary activity: the bishops from all over the world and the superiors of the various institutions and papal organizations. "They must meet at fixed times in order to exercise, under the authority of the pope, the supreme direction of the whole field of missionary activity." [29]

(b) The congregation will be assisted by a standing secretariat of scientific and missionary experts. This body must, among other things, be *au courant* with the situation in the various countries, the thought and sensibilities of the various human societies and the possible methods of evangelization; it must submit scientifically sound proposals that correspond with both the work in the mission field and that done in the mother countries insofar as the mission is concerned.

The organization of the *Propaganda Fide*, which has prevailed up until now, has reached a venerable age. It is headed by a cardinal prefect. He is assisted by a college of cardinals who, in the more important cases, give their advice and share in making decisions so that they really form the most important body of

[29] "Hi omnes, statutis temporibus convocandi, sub auctoritate Summi Pontificis supremam ordinationem totius operis missionalis exerceant" (*Decree on the Church's Missionary Activity*, n. 29).

the congregation. In practice, however, only those cardinals are
called in that are resident in Rome. Another important position
is that of the secretary general who represents the cardinal prefect. When more difficult questions have to be decided, a fair
number of consultors can be called upon, taken from the hierarchy or from the regular or secular clergy. To all this must be
added secretaries and clerical staff.

The request made by the Commission on the missions, and
adopted by the Council fathers, may be met sufficiently if this
noble apparatus is given a new vitality and expansion, more in
harmony with the demands of the time. The secretarial body of
experts, which consists of an active team of missiologists, soci-
ologists, pastoral theologians, ethnologists, etc., and people who
have missionary experience, might not altogether be a substitute
for the body of consultors, but it would be well suited to provide
them with most valuable material on which to base their decisions. In the view of the Council fathers the personnel of the
Propaganda Fide should not consist of functionaries who, in all
loyalty, rise from the ranks in the hope of climbing the professional ladder, but rather of those who would have enough understanding, zest and prudence to grasp the meaning of the required
measures and to carry them out. Above all, and again in the
view of the Council fathers, the kernel of that central authority,
the college mentioned above, should be far more representative
and truly reflect the world mission in the many-sided aspects of
its task; only such a body could believably have the insight and
impact required by the present situation in world, Church and
mission.

4. Until now an important part in the organization of the
world mission has been played by those bodies that represented
Rome in various mission countries, namely, the apostolic delega-
tions and internunciatures. These represented the Holy See in
their respective countries and their function was to inform the
Holy See about the state of Christianity there, to uphold the
interests of the Church, to make decisions on urgent problems
put to them, to link the younger (local) Churches with Rome,

to lift missionary work out of its isolation, to encourage co-operation between various missions, and so on.

The *aggiornamento* of these institutions, too, has been discussed. If the *Decree on the Church's Missionary Activity* does not mention this, the reason may be that in the comprehensive perspective of the Council this question should be dealt with on the level of the regional conferences of the bishops or religious superiors and that of the curiae of the local Churches, *i.e.*, of the resident bishops. To enter into details here is beyond the scope of this article. The guiding principles, however, would still be the same: a dynamic direction, with a wider vision and broader cooperation, making use of trained and experienced teams of specialists. Hence, the suggestions of a "pastoral council" for the episcopal curia, of making the episcopal conferences and the co-operation among several episcopal conferences more effective, of more cooperation among the various missionary institutes— all this again is based on the recognized fact that the isolated institute or bishop is no longer equipped to deal with the demands of our time.

5. If so much has been said about organization, administration, planning, direction, method, *aggiornamento*, and so on, we must conclude that all this may indeed be very useful and even necessary and that man must indeed serve God's work with all his abilities, but that all this is in the end not the decisive element.

If God does not build the house, the laborers labor in vain. Missionary work is at heart a work of grace, and, therefore, a work of God, a work of the Holy Spirit. The Holy Spirit decides the hour. It depends on him whether our human laboring and planning and worrying will lead to the communication of grace. But it is also characteristic of his dispensation to choose the weak in order to confound the strong or even to do without the human element altogether, and thus bring about grace and conversion.

Saul was full of anger and the lust to kill, and the Lord's disciples kept nervously out of his way, but the light of grace struck him and the voice of the Lord called out to him: "Saul,

Saul, why do you persecute me?" Peter refused to speak and share the table with the pagan Cornelius, but the messenger of the Lord said to Cornelius: "Your prayers and your alms have ascended as a memorial before God." The "apostles and elders in Jerusalem" were full of zeal for the work of the Lord, but God convinced them through the signs and wonders he worked through Paul and Barnabas among the Gentiles "that they should not trouble those of the Gentiles who turn to God". A sharp contention arose on account of John Mark between Paul and Barnabas, and they worked no longer as a team, but God continued to use them as his instruments. At heart, the mission is the work of God. Not without reason did the Lord add to his missionary command the promise: "Lo, I am with you always, to the close of the age."

Walbert Bühlmann, O.F.M.Cap./*Fribourg, Switzerland*

The African Church: The Council of Jerusalem to Vatican Council II

To attempt a survey cuts both ways. One covers everything and nothing, and then still falls victim to self-deception because although one thinks he knows it all, he can but indicate events, not really deal with them. We may at least get around one obstacle and try not to limit ourselves to what is mere façade and outward development of the Church in Africa but rather keep our eye on both the magnetic poles which dominate the inner life of this Church.

When the whole Church tries to grapple with her aggiornamento, her inward renewal, to rejuvenate herself by throwing off the crusts and torpidity accumulated in the course of the centuries, and to face confrontation and contact with the original forces of her origin, the Church of Africa, too, must share in the process, for it is a part of the whole Church and in many ways reflects this encrusted Western Church. Therefore, it cannot, any more than the rest, avoid the purpose of Vatican Council II: the inner renewal of the Church.

But, apart from this 20th-century task, there still remains the 1st-century task, the aims of the Council of Jerusalem: the disengagement from its predecessor, the Synagogue, the progressive penetration into a wide, non-Christian world and the confrontation with this world. These specifically missionary problems have understandably received less attention at Vatican Council II.* They belong to the post-conciliar tasks of the episcopal conferences in an Africa where the Church still resembles that of the Council of Jerusalem.

Before we take a closer look at these two aspects, we must have a framework in which this whole historical event fits and briefly outline the outward appearance of this African Church. The first missionary opportunity in Africa, which covers the first seven centuries, opened with great promise in North Africa and ended in total fiasco. The second opportunity came during the 16th-18th centuries in the Congo and other regions of Central and West Africa with the same result. The third missionary period is the present. It began in the middle of the last century and is therefore the shortest, though at the same time also the most successful. After decades of pioneering there was an increasingly rapid growth in the number of Catholics. In the regions subject to the *Propaganda Fide* (Sacred Congregation for Propagating the Faith), there were 4,526,095 Catholics in 1927, 6,794,951 in 1938, 18,896,649 in 1955, and 24,262,266 in 1963. If we include the catechumens who number about 3 million and take the whole of Africa, the Catholic population today numbers over 30 million. There are about 2,700 African priests and more than 6,000 African sisters (exact numbers are not obtainable since statistics no longer differentiate between black and white where priests and religious are concerned). At the end of the third session of the Council, *i.e.*, in the autumn of 1964, there were 16 African archbishops and 50 African bishops. This African Church is now confronted with the tensions and tasks that confronted the first and the last Councils in the history of the Church.[1]

---

* EDITORIAL NOTE: This article was sent in the month of July, 1965, that is, before the Schemas on the Church's Missionary Activity and on Non-Christian Religions had been accepted and published.

[1] For more about the external development and the internal problems, cf. W. Bühlmann, *Afrika, gestern, heute, morgen* (Herder Bücherei, n. 86; 2nd ed.: Freiburg im Br., 1961); Spanish ed.: Herder (Barcelona, 1964); *idem, Die Kirche unter den Völkern—Afrika* (Matthias Grüne-

I

RENEWAL FROM WITHIN

Nemo dat quod non habet—no one can give what he does not have. Fifty or twenty years ago missionaries went out to the African missions with a religious education and youthful impressions that went some fifteen years farther back. With just these impressions, ideals and methods, they preached Christianity in Africa. These ways and means might well have served their purpose in the "good old days", in Europe as well as in Africa (otherwise the missionaries themselves would never have become the good, zealous Christians they were), but today these ways are no longer adequate, either in Europe or in Africa. While in the missionaries' home countries the many-sided renewal, fully accepted by the Council, had made headway (at least officially), the African Church has only recently linked up with this movement, and mainly so since the Council. It is good to see how in Africa, too, the face of the Church has changed today and how the aims of Vatican Council II are beginning to take shape.

1. *Catechetical Renewal*

The 30 million African Catholics have been instructed in their faith mainly by means of the "Small Catechism". In the beginning the educational system was so little developed that nothing could be done except learn it by heart. Even today there are still many districts where the catechists still cannot read or write, and so they simply teach the others the questions and answers of the catechism that they themselves know backwards. Many of these catechisms have been constantly reprinted without change for the last fifty years.

Yet, here and there the renewal has set in during the last two or three decades. In particular, the International Study Week on

wald Verlag, Mainz, 1963; French ed.: Desclée Cie, Tournai, 1965; Eng. ed.: Sheed & Ward, London, 1966); J. Mullen, *The Catholic Church in Modern Africa* (Chapman, London, 1965); C. Groves, *The Planting of Christianity in Africa* I-IV (Lutterworth Press, London, 1958).

Missionary Catechetics in Eichstätt (1960) has given a powerful impetus to it. Its extensive report[2] has been sent free to all missionary bishops. Since then there has been growing unrest everywhere, and groups or individuals have supported a movement to revise their catechetical textbooks and methods. The same purpose was served by the Pan-African Catechetical Study Week in Katigondo, Uganda (August 26–September 1, 1964). This had been decided upon by the African bishops as a result of their first meeting during the Council. Fr. Johannes Hofinger, S.J., was entrusted with its organization. Twenty-seven experts from Europe and America and seventy-two bishops, priests and lay people from sixteen African countries took part in it. A common attempt was made to get a clear view of the situation and to suggest the necessary measures. The papers, discussions and resolutions were printed in several pastoral periodicals *in extenso*.[3] They will make their contribution to provide Africa with a catechetical method which may help the African of today to make up his mind and thus bring about a real change.

This Study Week had two noteworthy results. The desire was expressed to promote and coordinate information and research and establish a center for this purpose for the whole of Africa. The White Fathers then decided to extend their *Centre de Pastorale Catéchétique et Liturgique* in Butare, Rwanda, for this purpose, and placed it under the direction of Fr. X. Seumois. The contacts made in Katigondo also led to picking up the threads in connection with the excellent catechism for adults, *Africa's Way to Life*,[4] which had appeared in South Africa in 1963, and to offering it to other regions so that missionaries everywhere would not have to waste time in doing the same thing. At present it is being translated into fourteen different African languages, and will then be printed by Geoffrey Chapman in London at one

[2] *Katechetik heute,* ed. J. Hofinger (Herder, Freiburg im Br., 1961; Eng. Tr.: *Teaching All Nations* (Herder & Herder, New York).

[3] *African Ecclesiastical Review* (Masaka in Uganda, Oct. 1964); *Revue du Clergé africain,* special number (Mayidi in Congo); *Teaching All Nations* (Hongkong, Oct. 1964).

[4] In three volumes (Department of Education and Catechetics of the South African Catholic Bishops' Conference, Pretoria).

time. The Lenten Campaign of the Swiss Catholics will bear half the expense so that the African missions can afford this comprehensive catechism with color illustrations.

A special principle for the future will have to be that mere teaching will change into dialogue while more use is made of pre-Christian values as a starting point so that Christianity is planted not just in the mind but in the whole concrete existence of man. Here Fr. P. Tempels, O.F.M., has pointed the way both in theory and in practice.[5]

2. Biblical Renewal

The word has an astounding power in Africa. The word of the witch doctor was infallible to the old Africans. The word of a political leader casts a spell over the masses. The word of the neo-African writer fascinates the readers. The magic of the word is considered an essential element of neo-African culture.[6] One can imagine how the power of the Word of God could radiate here, and how the Africans would react to such a kerygma.

We must frankly admit that the Protestant missions have been far ahead of us in this spreading of the Word of God: not that we did not do anything, but the fact remains that we are far behind. Today we realize that—from a catechesis, the renewal of which should lead to the Sacred Scriptures, and from the renewal of a liturgy that begins with the celebration of the Word —there is a pressing need for a translation of the Bible into the various African languages. However, it would have been an irresponsible waste of energy and personnel if, merely for the sake of prestige and because of an out-of-date anti-Protestant attitude, we started to do all over again what the Protestants had already done. Accordingly, discussions took place in 1962 between Catholic and Protestant missionaries in the regions where Swahili is spoken. This led to the following result: Catholics would take over the present text of the Protestant Bible, adding the deutero-

---

[5] Cf. his new book, *Notre Rencontre* (Leopoldville, 1962).
[6] Cf. J. Jahn, *Muntu; Umrisse der neoafrikanischen Kultur* (Düsseldorf, 1958), esp. pp. 125-59.

canonical books and whatever footnotes would be considered necessary. But this was only a first step toward a quick spreading of the Bible. As a second step, a commission was appointed, composed of both Catholics and Protestants who would together work out a revision of the text; this may take from eight to ten years. Then the Protestants will presumably take over this Bible together with the deutero-canonical books and the footnotes so that there will be one and the same Bible for all.

This Tanzanian precedent has found followers. Today a similar collaboration has been planned or set in motion in several African countries, and in order to further this development, the following resolution was adopted at the Study Week of Katigondo: "Considering the common love of Holy Writ, which binds all Christians together, and in view of the present ecumenical endeavor and the unquestionable need of a Holy Writ in the vernacular, the Pan-African Catechetical Study Week begs the hierarchy of all parts of Africa to make contact with the Protestant authorities wherever this is indicated in order to provide a speedy and common publication of the Old and the New Testaments in translations that are exegetically and linguistically unexceptionable. In the meantime we recommend that, with the approval of the hierarchy, Catholics will be allowed to use the Protestant Bible." [7]

3. *The Liturgical Renewal*

The celebration of Mass has always been a communal action in Africa. The so-called "silent" Mass simply did not exist. People prayed and sang in common whatever they knew by heart. But while there was a certain variety in the sung parts of the Mass, the prayers remained the same year in, year out, with stereotyped passages for the *Introit*, the *Gloria* and even for the *Epistle* and *Gospel*, and so on. The increasing number of translated missals and the liturgical renewal indicate here, too, a chance to exploit

[7] Cf. the series of articles "Die Bibel in der kath. Weltmission," in *N. Zeitschr. f. Missionsw.* (Schöneck-Beckenried, 1960-5; also published in book form by NZM.

the latest possibilities. The African is by nature wholly in tune with liturgical action. He is less inclined than the Indian to sit down on the temple floor and lose himself in meditation. The African is an extrovert. He loves to look at color, pictures and symbols together, to listen, pray and sing together, and to sit, stand and act together. He does not grope and brood, but lives intuitively and existentially. When Africans sing their religious songs and perform their rites, the music radiates and resounds. When the liturgical renewal gets under way, we shall be surprised by Africa's contribution now that the way for local adaptation stands open.

In the meantime progress is still quiet. Fr. Boniface Luykx, O. Praem., for example, is busy in Leopoldville with a working group studying the various elements of African piety and their possible exploitation for the liturgy, so that it can really become a "celebration" that appeals to the African. Recently an African priest, B. Nyom, has pointed out in a dissertation that the African way of praying is wholly existential, rooted in the concrete historical situation, and develops as a dramatic happening that involves man, the tribe and the whole of creation in a communal, liturgical form. Consequently, the prayer formulas which the catechumens learn by heart and recite every Sunday—e.g., morning prayers, the ten commandments, the acts of faith, hope and charity before each Mass!—impoverish the religious temperament of the African.[8] Hopefully, the liturgical renewal will put a stop to this impoverishment.

4. Dialogue

The period of colonization was marked by the monologue. Even the missionary easily fell victim (despite his heroic attitude) to that paternalism which may have been necessary at the

---

[8] "Prière biblique et prière négro-africaine," in Mélanges de Science Religieuse XXI (Lille, 1964), pp. 32-99. "Since the Bantu prayer is a performance rather than a meditation, they concentrate on their attitude more than on the formula" (p. 94). "In Africa, the ready-made prayer, without any attempt at adaptation, has paralyzed and impoverished the religious expression of the African Negro" (p. 95).

start but was nevertheless a mistake from the pedagogical point of view. One did everything for the African, but that did not involve him. At the first international congress of African authors and artists in Paris (1956), one speaker said: "The world is divided into two camps, the camp of the loudspeakers and the camp of the silent mouths. For centuries the European sang his solo part and filled the earth with his commands." [9] Even African priests wrote in their first collective publication: "For too long people have tackled our problems for us, without us and even against us." [10] The revolution in Africa, the spirit of Pope John and that of the Council urgently demand a dialogue in Africa, too.

(a) *The Dialogue with African Catholics.* In the secular field the Africans have taken over responsibility at a surprising pace. This has had a beneficial effect on African priests and bishops. True, the Church was at an advantage in this field, for she already had dioceses independently governed by African bishops and priests when no country had as yet attained political independence. De-colonization and the consequent Africanization in politics and economics stimulated the promotion of African forces within the Church. The African bishops, priests and lay people, who until then believed that they were considered less important than the missionaries, now visibly assume full responsibility and direction. Before this the Church was widely thought of as the affair of the missionaries. Now the Africans realize that she is "their" Church. To bring lay people into action at every level— in the parochial council, in Catholic Action, as catechists, for Christian education of children within the family, in public life, and the training which all this requires—is today a predominant concern.

The sixth episcopal conference held at Leopoldville-Congo in 1961 frequently dealt with the new situation and the problems arising from it. In connection with this it declared: "In order to discover, encourage and train vocations to the priesthood and to

---

[9] *Présence Africaine* (Paris, 1956), p. 21.
[10] *Des Prêtres noirs s'interrogent* (Ed. du Cerf, Paris, 1956), p. 16.

religious life, the Church in the Congo has made tremendous efforts and heavy sacrifices. In the future the lay apostolate must be given equally decisive importance. The priest must therefore do everything to stimulate lay vocations, to train Christians who will take up the apostolate and to maintain the zeal of those who have already given of their best to this apostolate." [11]

(b) *Dialogue with Protestant Fellow Christians.* As within Protestantism, the ecumenical movement sprang from the missions because there the division into many Churches and sects was still more disastrous than in the homeland; yet the *rapprochement* between Catholics and Protestants needs more time there than in Europe and America. The reason is that in the missions both groups are at the head of the march and this creates rivalry, while in the West they live side by side in a position of stability. In spite of this, the "Johannine Era" has suddenly dawned also in Africa.

The present situation in Africa presents the Churches with the plain alternative of either working together over a wide field or capitulating. For when two parties are quarreling, the third one is quite happy, and this third party is materialism, communism and Islam. If the Churches do not manage to work together at a social level in their fight against alcoholism, prostitution and corruption, they will all be equally powerless. If they cannot make the common influence of all Christians and believers bear on political life, then they will be responsible for the fact that politics will shake off all contact with religion. And if, in matters concerning the Church, they cannot give the impression of a certain unity, then they will not be able to prevent more and more baptized Christians from turning away from the Church; they will not be able to stop the process of increasing disintegration, or win over a population that is rapidly emancipating itself from the old paganism.

Accordingly, much has improved during recent years in relations between the Churches, and many things are happening that give cause for joy. For instance, the World Unity Octave is cele-

[11] *Actes* (Leopoldville, 1961), p. 197.

brated together; there is not only mutual collaboration in the translation of the Bible but there are also Bible Weeks held in common, and in the matter of schools they no longer fight each other but plan together and together defend the rights of the denominational school against the governments. In Cameroon an interdenominational organization was founded recently for the apostolate of the film. An interdenominational committee in the U.S.A. gave an airplane to the missionaries of all denominations in Kenya. It is marked with a dove, the symbol of peace, and bears the initials U.M.A.T.T. (United Missionary Air Training and Transport). It is hoped that a second airplane will soon follow and that the service will be extended to other countries. With regard to the common exploitation of mass media, the Katigondo Study Week adopted a resolution begging the hierarchy, in view of Catholic collaboration, to approach the Lutheran radio station, "The Voice of the Gospel", at Addis Ababa, which provides excellent programs. On the other hand, with the help of the K.R.O. (the Dutch Radio and Television Center) and the *Misereor* movement of Germany, it is hoped to set up a powerful transmitting station in Liberia that will be open to all Christians in Africa.

5. *Local Churches*

The Council has proposed, also in view of the missions, to proceed to a far-reaching decentralization of the Church and has increased the importance of the local episcopal conferences. The African Church was not altogether unprepared for this increase in responsibility. There were already twenty national episcopal conferences, of which several have well-organized secretariats that function smoothly. The 300 African bishops surprised everybody at the Council when they were the first to set up a continental general secretariat under the presidency of Cardinal Laureano Rugambwa, assisted by two general secretaries, Archbishop Zoa for the French-speaking section and Bishop Blomjous for the English-speaking section. Moreover, the twenty national conferences have combined into nine regional conferences so that there is more room for planning and action. Consequently, the Church appears throughout as the one Catholic Church, but at the same time as the Church of Africa, the Church with 300 dioceses and about 5,000 main missionary stations, in all of which the Church exists and grows.

The outward appearance of the Church is becoming visibly more African in shape and color. It is true that since Benedict XV the popes had laid down clear principles for this adaptation, but these remained principles and theories that were not put into practice. Not until the rise of African nationalism were these principles taken seriously and did one realize that the Church must incarnate the values that are peculiar to each people. Today many things are being done. Until a few years ago the people sang, almost without exception, European hymns with a translated text; now there is a veritable spring of African songs for use in church. Church decoration, illustrated catechisms and prayer books, the display of the liturgy—all these things now strive more and more toward an African style.

Before the opening of the Council the *Société Africaine de Culture* sent out hundreds of questionnaires to bishops, priests and lay people in Africa in order to provoke a clear reaction to the subject of "The Catholic Church and African Culture" and so to influence the Council. Unfortunately only a few replies were received. However, in a Roman seminary, in May 1963, a group of African priests and lay people discussed these questions and published the results.[12]

When the Africans have become Christian, Christianity must also become African, not merely in order to involve the whole man but also in order not to hamper the contemporary African witness more than is necessary.

[12] "Personnalité africaine et Catholicisme," in *Présence Africaine* (Paris, 1963).

II

THE CHURCH AND THE SOCIETY THAT SURROUNDS IT

As part of the 2,000-year-old Church, the African Church must not only rejuvenate and revitalize itself with reference to the original image—which was the main purpose of Vatican Council II—but must as a young Church face up to the same problems that the early Church and the Council of Jerusalem had to face. It must confront the society that surrounds it, exercise its mission in it and examine its relationship with this society. Although the christianization of a human person or a whole people is a process that can never be completed, there are, nevertheless, problems that are peculiar to the start of this process. The African Church is a Church at its beginning, a Church of neophytes. By far the majority of its 30 million followers are Christians of the first or second generation. Bishop Anastasius Hartmann, O.F.M.C. (1803-66), who before his appointment in India was professor at the missionary college of St. Fidelis in Rome, wrote a book on pastoral work in the mission[13] and devoted a special chapter on how to deal with neophytes. What is surprising is not just his sensitive insight into the rather special situation of the neophytes but also the fact that he counts as such all those whose Christian ancestors do not go back more than 200 years!

1. *The Missionary in the World*

The Protestant historian of the missions, K. S. Latourette, called the period of the latest revival of missionary activity "the greatest century" in the history of Christianity,[14] and by that he means principally the mission in Africa. Nowhere and at no time was an indigenous Church so quickly founded and built up as

---

[13] *Psychologia arti pastorali applicata*, ed. A. Jann (Innsbruck, 1914). Cf. especially ch. 8. See also W. Bühlmann, *Ein Pionier der Einheit: Bisschof Anastasius Hartmann* (Schöningh, Paderborn, 1966).

[14] *History of the Expansion of Christianity* VI (seven vols., New York, 1937-45), p. 442.

on this continent. In several African countries 25% to 50% of the population are Catholics. And since most of these Christians belong to the younger generation and the older people remain pagan, the Catholic population increases proportionately every year, even apart from new conversions. In many places there will be a Christian majority within ten or twenty years, and in this sense the population explosion works in favor of Christians, while in Asia Christians are reduced to a diminishing minority.

The rapid expansion of Christianity is the more urgent as African religions show a rapid decline, in spite of certain revivals. They carry the seed of decay within them, for they are definitely tribal religions. The head of the tribe is also the religious head, and the graves of the ancestors are the place where religion is practiced. When, however, the tribe breaks up—and this is what is happening—the sacrifices to the ancestors cease, and so do the initiation rites and the remaining religious customs. They are also what one might call "integral" religions in the sense that *everything* is permeated by religion and given a religious significance. The spirits—the "first causes"—are responsible for the health and fruitfulness in the family and in the field. "Secondary causes" hardly count at all. But as people begin to think in terms of causality, technology and science—for which every school is a radiating center—the tribal religion is faced with a crisis to which it will succumb. The microbes are replacing the spirits. Instead of placing fetishes in the field, people now try to obtain seed of better quality. Instead of praying for strength to live, they now buy pills. To sum up, in contrast with the advanced cultural religions of Asia, primitive religions have no real founders, no prophets, no holy books, no supra-tribal organization, and so they disintegrate before the assault of this new age. If Christianity fails to provide a home for these masses as they turn away from paganism, Africa will suffer from a catastrophic spiritual vacuum.

The African Church, then, faces a gigantic task, but it has also had an astounding success which has maintained itself since its newly achieved independence. But the Church is well aware of the fact that its task is by no means fulfilled merely by the initial preaching, and there is an increasing demand that the emphasis must now shift from expansion to work in depth. These two tasks do not exclude each other. A Church that has passed through a genuine inner renewal will know from understanding its own nature that it must of necessity be a missionary Church. Nor can it rest content with what has been achieved; it will have to leave the pentecostal room and bear witness with an active laity and more vocations to the priesthood. As this comes about, the African Church will, with the Church as a whole, prefer to speak of a "missionary renewal" rather than of a "missionary movement". The mission will no longer be looked on as just outward activity and growing achievement, but will rather be recognized as an inner attitude that penetrates a Christian's whole thought, prayer and action, shaping all this and making it truly Christian. The mission releases forces that lead to the inner renewal of the Church and to the highest forms of the Christian apostolate. In this way the mission stands on the same level as the liturgical movement and the scriptural movement which are also a renewal and which, together with the missionary renewal, share a mutual interdependence.

2. The "Alien" Character of Christianity in Africa

In spite of all the successes, one should not indulge in illusions. Christianity has a certain prestige in Africa. Thanks to its schools, most civilized and responsible people are Christian. It remains, nevertheless, in many ways, and more than we realize, an alien organization in contemporary Africa, just like early Christianity in the Roman Empire. During the colonization period the Church was still more at its beginning than it is today. Preaching took place within the framework of European colonial government. The missionaries were principally, and for a long time, European missionaries. After an initial opposition, most Africans became keen on imitating the Europeans in dress, in culture, in standards of living, in wealth and, understandably, in religion. The cultural ideal of Europe seemed to them a desirable paradise. During this period it was easy to introduce into Africa Western forms of preaching, liturgy, Church music, Church architecture, etc. Consequently, the Church of Rome found itself at home in Africa, while the Africans accepted this Western context of the Church without thinking too much about it.

But with World War II, a change set in. There was an awakening of national awareness which set off the process of decolonization with increased speed. Within the space of a few years no less than thirty-five new States came into being. Today the European, whether he be technician, businessman or missionary, is but a guest in a foreign country. As a result, the European atmosphere of the Church, already mentioned, suddenly became a questionable asset, and this affected what was until then the unquestioned authority of the missionary and the predominantly negative attitude toward the African, *i.e.*, "pagan" tradition.

Suddenly the missionary Church of the West realized that it was living in a strange world from the point of view of religion. Just as the early Church had to try to detach herself from her predecessor, the Synagogue, in order to make things no more difficult for the converts from paganism than was really necessary, so the present-day African Church must try to detach itself from its predecessor, the Western Church, so that the Africans do not have to carry a heavier burden of Western historical elements than is required. For the sake of brevity I am not going to deal with these outward European aspects in detail but I will rather concentrate on the inward tension that has arisen between the preaching of Christianity and the traditions of Africa.

There is, of course, no way of devaluating or watering down the essence of the kerygma. One cannot avoid the "scandal of the cross". The religious shock in the moment of faith, the conversion to Christ, must not be softened down by present catechetical methods, but, on the contrary, made more intense. The problem is rather how much "scandal of the law" should be imposed and with how many Western attitudes—which have in many ways already been proved out of date—the Africans should be saddled.

This is what an African bishop referred to when he said to the

Council reporter, Fr. L. Kaufman, S.J.: "You see, we are just good enough to help old Europe to clear up its own affairs. We sit here and help with our votes to patch up a situation of the Church that has come about in Europe's past and to find here and there a way out. But when I began to realize this during the second session, I spent three weeks in prayer and meditation to find out whether I should say 'yes' to a past that is not ours, and out of a feeling of solidarity should deny an honest desire to do away with what is really obstructive. . . . But what I expected of the Council was to know what is relative and conditioned by historical circumstances, and what is the kernel, what is the Gospel I have to preach on our continent." [15]

It seemed obvious to the Europeans that from the start all "pagan" practices should be condemned and forbidden to all Christians. But as the Christians lived, and still live, in an environment that is half or more than half non-Christian, and since life there is impregnated by religion, these Christians cannot ignore the religious life of the tribe. One would have to enclose them in glass or completely isolate them, and even then they would carry many "pagan" convictions and practices with them. In fact, and in spite of decades of unequivocal prohibitions, many Christians still participate more or less in the religious life of the tribe. This puts them in a permanent dilemma. As an African priest, James Komba, now bishop of Songea in Tanzania, put it in his dissertation: "On this point I can speak from my own experience. What a burden it is to a young Ngoni Christian when he does not know what attitude to take in this pagan environment. In every pagan rite he detects an occasion of sin. He is pulled into opposite directions by two powerful forces, parental authority and Church authority. It seems to him that the Church has nothing else to offer than a 'Thou shalt not'. When, for instance, the older people invite him to a ritual meal, he thinks he has to partake of it. He eats against his conscience, and then regrets having done it. And so, in his mind, the world appears to be simply a load of 'scandal'. Consequently, he comes

[15] *Hochland* 57 (Feb. 1965), p. 208.

to the opinion that Christianity has nothing good and nothing joyful to offer." [16]

We really ought to ask ourselves whether this problem should not be completely reexamined. The African religions, with their predominant monotheism and their set world-image of the power of life, through studies in comparative religion have proven to be very different from what we thought they were during the last four centuries since the age of discovery. This demands, therefore, a fresh theological assessment, in line with the whole theological rethinking of the place of non-Christian religions.[17] Missionary practice cannot afford to ignore this reassessment by theology and comparative religion. A convert from paganism should not suddenly condemn what up till then was his legitimate religion. Fully realizing that he has progressed from a provisional religion to a definitive one, he should continue to recognize the relative legitimacy of African religion and should be allowed to share in the expression of it within a certain setting, just as the apostles continued to visit the Synagogue, but celebrated their own eucharist over and above that.

In practice this means that the African convert from paganism should be allowed to take part in religious tribal customs, insofar as they are "religious" and do not directly offend against love, justice or morals. This would be the case, for instance, with the customary libations for the ancestors at harvest time or in cases of death, even when these rites are linked with wrong presentations about the character and needs of their ancestors' afterlife. These could be considered as "errors" such as occurred in the imperfect presentations we find in the Old Testament, which are not evil in themselves and can be given a right interpretation by the Christian, so that he will see in these libations simply an act of piety toward the ancestors and the tribe. He should also be

[16] *God and Man. Religious Elements of the Ngoni of South-West Tanganyika, Viewed in the Light of Christian Faith* (Pont. Urban. Univ. de Propaganda Fide, 1959), p. 264.

[17] I only refer to H. Schlette, *Die Religionen als Thema der Theologie* (Quaestiones disputatae, 22; Herder, Freiburg im Br., 1964) and its bibliography, and to *Gott in Welt. Festgabe K. Rahner* (Herder, Freiburg im Br., 1965), 2nd vol.

allowed to visit the elder of the tribe, the "witch doctor" as he is called, and ask for a medicine when his wife has no children, because in fact these "witch doctors" often have medicines that are effective; and if they link this with a reference to the ancestors and the stream of life that hails from them, there is again nothing in that which is evil in itself. Again, when a pagan "preacher" travels through the country in order to purge the people of black magic, the Christian should not be bluntly told that he cannot take part. In fact, most would go because otherwise they would be suspected of black magic.

This list should be carefully qualified and extended, and this can only be done through constant dialogue with genuine and open-minded Christians and their conscience. There are obviously pagan customs that are wrong in themselves. This leaves Christians no option but to oppose them, as only in this way can they be purged of this evil. Many other customs, particularly those connected with magic, contradict the whole modern progress of science, and these should be fought on that basis. It is, however, curious how long this thinking in terms of magic remains even with a modern African who is away from his tribe. Lastly, there are other customs that a Christian could and should share while interpreting them and changing them in the end into Christian customs. In all this, therefore, legalistic prohibitions lead nowhere as experience has shown. Only thorough theological penetration can bring clarity and provide a firm basis, and this shows that the business is not completed with catechism instruction. Only an intensive formation of adults, a constant deepening of the faith and a constantly new realization that the Old Testament and the pre-Christian African religions have been basically superseded can create adult Christians for whom there is no danger of syncretism and who will not destroy anything essentially religious in the pre-Christian African.

It is still interesting to see how St. Paul dealt with this kind of question. Jewish Christians attacked him because he did not impose the law and circumcision on pagans who offered themselves for baptism. The Council of Jersualem approved of this practice of his and declared that converts from paganism should not be burdened with a yoke that one could not bear oneself, and that these converts obtained salvation through the grace of the Lord Jesus. James, however, still insisted on four partly legalistic restrictions: they should abstain from sacrificing to idols, from blood, from what was strangled and from unchastity (Acts 15, 1-35). Insofar as the food offered to idols is concerned, Paul made a stand, but at a deeper level of theological understanding. In 1 Corinthians 10, 14-20, his argument runs in the form of a syllogism as follows: In Judaism, as in Christianity and in paganism, the sacrifice creates a community. "Are not those who eat the sacrifices partners in the altar?" But, "what the pagans sacrifice they offer to demons and not to God." Therefore, "I do not want you to be partners with demons. . . . You cannot partake of the table of the Lord and the table of demons." If, however, the minor term in this syllogism is no longer valid in view of the new light thrown upon this matter by comparative religion and theology, then the whole question has to be thought out anew. In this brief article I can only give some indications.

The new theological insight obviously also demands an element of pastoral understanding. Is it sound to bring a sudden change into what has been the practice in this matter so far? Are the majority of Christians already adult enough to understand and to know what to do? St. Paul knew about the consideration due to the weaker and less enlightened among the Christians. Although he did not agree with taking part in idolatrous sacrifices, he nevertheless thought it was permissible to buy sacrificial meat in the market and to eat it, since it had no longer any connection with the ritual act. But if this would shock others, he felt one should forego it out of charity. Otherwise, "by your knowledge this weak man is destroyed, the brother for whom Christ died. Thus, sinning against your brethren and wounding their conscience when it is weak, you sin against Christ. . . . Therefore, if food is a cause of my brother's falling, I will never eat meat, lest I cause my brother to fall" (1 Cor. 8, 7-13). It is therefore wholly a matter of sound explanation and a mature conscience, which will, however, ultimately be swayed by love.[18]

And so, there are still many controversial issues to be solved which up till now emphasized the non-African character of Christianity, and which could possibly be handled differently if there were a period of dialogue, just as dialogue has taken the edge off many controversial issues with Protestantism, so that they have even become acceptable to both sides. In any case, "the wish for a *Confessio Africana* is understandable, not in view of formulating a new dogmatic creed, but in order to find an answer to the specific problems of the African Christian, based on the Gospel and the existing creed".[19]

Finally, in spite of all this justified and necessary concern with the African environment and the consequent Africanization of Christianity, one should never forget that there is a "contradiction" between the essence of the Christian message and the "world" in the biblical sense. And so, the African Christian, too, will have to muster the courage to realize that he is "a pilgrim and a stranger" and that in the meantime he cannot escape the "strange" character of his existence.

[18] Cf. Y. Congar, *Sacerdoce et laïcat* (Ed. du Cerf, Paris, 1962).
[19] E. Dammann, *Die Religionen Afrikas* (Stuttgart, 1963), p. 253.

Mark Fang Che-yong, S.J./*Baguio, Philippines*

Catholic Church in China: Present Situation and Future Prospects

Much has been written about China recently, particularly in English, French and German. A recent book by Thaddäus Hang[1] gives a fairly complete picture of the Catholic Church in China, full of information and containing an extensive bibliography. In this article I propose to present the principal data about the present situation of Catholic missions and then concentrate on two main points: the situation of Catholicism under Chinese communism and the problem of adaptation.

I

THE ACTUAL SITUATION OF CATHOLICISM IN CHINA

Continental China

When the Communist regime came to power the total population was 461 million, of whom 3,295,658 were Catholics— an increase of 20,948 over the previous year, 1948.[2] The clergy

[1] T. Hang, "Die katholische Kirche im chinesischen Raum," Geschichte und Gegenwart (Sammlung Wissenschaft und Gegenwart) (Munich, 1963).

[2] I am indebted to Rev. J. Drahl, S.J. who allowed me to use this data from an article he has written for *The New Catholic Encyclopedia*, (Washington, Catholic University of America). For further figures, see *China News Analysis* (CNA) 186 (Hong Kong) June 28, 1957.

consisted of 96 bishops, 5,701 priests, 978 monks and 1,927 nuns, 874 senior and 2,659 junior seminarians. There were three Catholic universities: Fujen in Peking, founded in 1925, with 2,324 students in 1950 (407 Catholic and 1,917 non-Catholic); Tsinku in T'ientsin, founded in 1923 as a higher institute of industry and commerce, with 887 students (86 Catholic and 801 non-Catholic); Aurora in Shanghai, founded in 1903, with 1,472 students (414 Catholic and 1,058 non-Catholic). There were also 202 secondary schools with 53,306 pupils and 1,849 primary schools with 183,233 pupils and also some 2,000 catechism classes.

The *Annuario Pontificio* (1965) keeps the same hierarchical division of 15 years ago (cf. pp. 1250-51): 20 archdioceses, 93 dioceses, 29 apostolic prefectures. But more than 70 of the ordinaries of these sees are known to have been expelled from China for being foreigners. Of these more than 12 are now dead. Only Bishop J. Walsh, who on March 18, 1960, was condemned to 20 years imprisonment, remained in China. Bishop L. Bianchi of Hong Kong is also prevented from exercising his pastoral ministry over the greater part of his diocese on the far side of the Bamboo Curtain.

The 35 Chinese ordinaries consisted of 4 archbishops, 20 bishops, 3 apostolic prefects and 8 apostolic administrators. Of these, 5 bishops are known to have died, 5 were sentenced to prison after a popular trial, 4 without any trial and 7 more were prevented from exercising their ministries. A few bishops were outside China for particular reasons at the time of the Communist victory and have not been able to return to their sees.[3]

Catholic life in Communist China, if not absolutely impossible, is at least extremely precarious. Journalists who visited the country in 1965, such as Mark Gayn of the *Toronto Daily Star*[4] or Hans Henle of the *Suddeutsche Zeitung* (Munich), found little or nothing in the way of religious life to relate.

[3] Cf. T. Hang, *op. cit.* pp. 138-44.
[4] Cf. *The Philippines Herald* (Manila), June 14-20, 1965.

The latter reached a surprising credulity and ingenuousness in the long series of articles published in that paper in April and May, 1964.[5] On the other hand, a French priest, Abbé R. Baron, who visited China in 1964, was able to make contact with a Chinese priest from whom he learned that Vatican Council II has absolutely no influence on the Church in China. Liturgy goes on as before; the name of St. Joseph has not been introduced into the canon, the shortened form of the "Corpus Christi" at the people's communion is not used, the epistle and the gospel are still read in Latin, etc.[6] The Church there seems to be frightened of any sort of change and this is understandable. If it is an absolute necessity for us to renew the life of the Church, for them the vital point is to keep the essentials that they still have left. Any renewal that they were unable to control would cause confusion and do more harm than good.

Taiwan and Hong Kong

If continental China with its lowered horizon offers no more than negative and disheartening data, the Church that flourishes in Taiwan and Hong Kong opens bright perspectives for the present and near future. However, no Chinese, unless he were shortsighted, could feel entirely happy with the status quo in the two islands, however flourishing the situation may appear to be, since his heart and eyes are continually turned to the continent, hanging on the fate of his hundreds of millions of compatriots. The central government in Taipei considers Taiwan a model province with its highly successful agrarian reform, its growing industry and continually increasing foreign trade; [7]

[5] A letter I received from Munich said of these articles, among other things: "My reaction was one of horror at the naivete of a man who believed everything he heard."

[6] Cf. *Eglise Vivante* 17 (1965), pp. 54-64; *Die Kathol. Missionen* 82 (1963), pp. 24-8.

[7] According to the *Central Daily News* (Taipei), July 1, 1965 (the first day after the cessation of American economic aid, which had lasted for fifteen years), in 1964 the increase in agricultural output was 9.6%, in industrial production, 28.8%; and there was a surplus of exports over imports of $21,000,000. Personal earnings increased by 7.3%, the equivalent of $150, while the cost of living rose by only 2.5%.

it would like to transplant and apply these experiences to a continental China freed from Communist occupation. The Church in Taiwan lives in a similar state of psychological tension. Although there is a heartening amount of apostolic work on the island and it yields abundant fruit, the Church in Taiwan looks beyond the narrow limits of the island, dreaming of the time when its present apostolate will be able to benefit the whole Chinese continent.

Taiwan

In 1945 there were only 9,389 Catholics on the island. Ten years later there were 48,517 and 265,564 in June, 1964. This means that Catholics are 2.34% of the total population of the island (11,883,523), while on the continent they never reached 1% of the whole population of the nation. Twenty years ago the whole island was only an apostolic prefecture with less than 50 priests. Today the hierarchy of the island consists of 1 archdiocese and 6 dioceses with 712 priests, 73 religious brothers and 716 nuns. There are 4 junior seminaries with a total of 182 seminarians, and 1 senior seminary for late vocations with 24 seminarians. The interdiocesan senior seminary of St. Thomas Aquinas in Taipei has been recently approved by the Holy See; under the direction of the new rector, Rev. Joseph Liu, the construction of the buildings is now under way and the work of the seminary is being organized. There are 355 mass centers with one or more resident priests and 669 with no resident priest. There are 17 colleges of secondary education with a total of 12,094 pupils, and one of higher education in Taichung with 997 students. Fujen University, recently restored in Taipei, has 447 students. Catholic lecturers teaching in various universities total 77. There are 24 student residencies, 170 hospitals, clinics and dispensaries scattered throughout the island, 5 primary schools with 1,650 pupils, 503 nurseries with a total of 42,003 infants.[8]

[8] Cf. *Catholic Directory of Taiwan* (Taipei), 1965.

Hong Kong

On October 1, 1964, the total population of the colony was estimated at about 3,500,000, of whom 220,280 were Catholics, that is, about 6% of the total population. Since there were 62,921 Catholics in 1954 and in 1948 only 33,848, the rate of progress can clearly be seen. There are 336 priests working in the colony, 120 religious brothers and 733 nuns. There are 23 senior seminarians (including 6 studying in Rome) and 97 junior seminarians. There are 46 centers with a resident priest and 72 churches.

There are three particularly noticeable aspects of the Catholic Church in Hong Kong:

1. *The Lay Apostolate.* There are as many as 25,374 members of Catholic associations, and during 1964 they instructed 3,334 people for baptism and prepared 1,752 for holy communion and 1,260 for confirmation. The same lay apostles in the course of the year made also 22,813 visits to Catholic families, 23,067 visits to non-Catholic families and 3,188 visits to hospitals, where they ministered to 15,089 patients. The degree of their own spiritual formation can be gauged from the fact that 6,585 members of Catholic associations made the Spiritual Exercises at least once in 1964.

2. *Social Works.* There are 39 units of *Caritas* and 4 social centers, 6 hospitals with 1,315 beds and 31 clinics and dispensaries. Between them during 1964 they treated 690,000 cases. There are all types of centers for the care of infants and children from nurseries, orphanages, food and play centers, to various clubs with recreation and reading rooms, etc., for older boys and girls. There are a large number of other special services such as the 18 kitchen centers, which every day serve 8,000 hot meals to underprivileged children, etc.

3. *Educational Institutes.* The increased scale of Catholic education since the end of the Sino-Japanese war has been very considerable: in 1946 there were only 12 Catholic schools with 8,650 pupils; in 1956 the number had grown to 135 with 47,503

pupils, and in 1964 to 192 with a total of 133,687 pupils. There are 26 nurseries, 94 primary schools, 38 secondary schools, 7 technical or commercial colleges and 27 evening institutes.[9] There are no accurate recent statistics from Macao, but in 1958 the population of this Portuguese colony was estimated at 200,000. The Hong Kong Catholic *Annuario* for 1965 gives the same figure. Between these dates, however, the number of Catholics has grown from 25,365 to 32,000, making up 16% of the population of the colony. The Church is also making progress here in education and social works.

The Chinese of the Diaspora

Besides Hong Kong and Taiwan (and Macao) there is a third group of Chinese who must be taken into account: the Chinese of the diaspora. Statistics of 1961 give[10] the number of Chinese outside China as 13,326,802. Most of them, 12,872,937, are in Southeast Asia, of whom 276,862 are Catholic. The rest are distributed as follows (with the number of Catholics in each area in parentheses): America, 378,825 (45,859); Oceania, 82,056 (16,555); Africa, 60,300 (22,175); Europe, 28,667 (2,305).[11]

In conclusion, outside continental China the Church's mission is spread over three major groups of Chinese who, although living in very different conditions, are all free to embrace the faith: those of Taiwan, Hong Kong, Macao and the diaspora. The total number of Chinese throughout the free world is therefore almost 30 million, of whom 854,491 are Catholics.

[9] Cf. Hong Kong Catholic Directory, 1965 (Hong Kong), 1965.
[10] Cf. T. Hang, *op. cit.* pp. 185-208. The apostolic visitor, a former missionary in China, C. von Melckebeke, has contributed greatly to the development of an overall view of the apostolate in the Chinese diaspora.
[11] These figures give an overall picture, but are not exact. Europe, for example, has been taken as England, Holland and France only, whereas there are Chinese in Italy, Spain, Germany and elsewhere who together add up to a sizeable total.

II

A More Detailed Look at the Church in Communist China

The so-called Movement of Triple Self-Sufficiency (Self-Support, Self-Propagation and Self-Government) which lasted from 1951 to 1955 is well known. It was in fact a movement of independence from Rome. The Chinese Church in its full strength resisted the movement resolutely and overcame it. The two representative heroes of the period were Fathers Beda Chang, S.J., and John Tung, who in the two great cities of Shanghai and Chungking respectively unmasked the Communist plots with true Christian daring, and, through their clear-sightedness and brave confession of faith, showed the Catholics of the whole nation the road they had to follow. This period ended with the detention of Bishop Ignatius Kung of Shanghai and many other bishops, priests and laymen from all parts of China who were arrested on September 8 and 26, 1955. Bishop Kung became a symbol of the attitude typical of Chinese Catholics in general, toward communism trying to infiltrate into the Church: an upright, energetic, uncompromising, mistrustful and apparently hostile attitude toward the Communist authorities and their approaches to the Church, however friendly in appearance.[12] The importance and value of such a firm Catholic line in the initial phases of the resistance against communism cannot be denied, but this attitude could not be long maintained since the line of confrontation between the two fronts was constantly changing in accordance with the usual Communist tactics, always artfully seeking new and more effective ways of bringing the rebellious Catholics to heel. This is what we are going to examine next.

The Chinese Communists learned two things from the failure of the Triple Self-Sufficiency Movement: first, that Catholics

[12] One example given is that Bishop Kung refused to take part in the parade on October 1, 1953, and also refused a visit—apparently a friendly one—from the then mayor of Shanghai, Mr. Ch'en Yi.

could not be asked to declare themselves totally independent of Rome, and secondly, that any positive results could only be obtained by going to the head, that is, the hierarchy. It was this conviction that brought the Patriotic Catholic Chinese Association into being. Its general lines were laid down in two preparatory sessions in January and July of 1956 and its structure completed in two more sessions in February and June of 1957, the last of which (June 17-July 15) was immediately followed by the General Assembly in Peking (July 15-Aug. 2) in which the Association was officially founded. What happened in the General Assembly in Peking can be summed up in a Chinese proverb: *T'on ch'uan yi mon* ("the two slept in the same bed but each had a different dream"). The official communiqués of the Peking government give only the Communist dream. For example, in the *People's Daily* (August 3, 1957), the conclusions of the Assembly were published in the following terms: "The 241 representatives of the 3 million Catholics (the representatives included 10 bishops and 200 priests; the rest were nuns and laymen, all from the ruling class)[13] from 26 provinces and more then 100 dioceses reached agreement on the following points: Chinese Catholics should encourage the patriotic spirit, participate positively in the building up of the socialism of the country and other patriotic activities, defend world peace and help the government to realize its policy of religious freedom." [14] As for relations with the Vatican, the same *People's Daily* goes on: "The Assembly decided that the Chinese Catholic Church should have its own independence and authority with its own hierarchy, that it could maintain purely religious relations with the Vatican curia provided these did not prejudice the interests of the country or its own independence and dignity, that is, that in dogmatic and moral doctrines, what it should believe and practice, it can obey the supreme pontiff but it ought, on the other hand, to break off

[13] Cf. *Free Pacific Magazine,* 50 (Saigon), Feb. 1951, published in Chinese, p. 85.
[14] Cf. *ibid.* 49 (Jan. 1961), p. 24.

definitely all types of political and economic relations with the Vatican curia." [15]

Fortunately, there is another Catholic witness to the General Assembly of Peking outside the Communist press, a Mr. Thomas.[16] Thanks to him we can learn the other dream, that of the Catholics who took part in the Assembly, a dream that can be summed up in a single preoccupation: to save whatever possible.[17] The facts were these:

1. The first net spread by the Communists consisted in making many bishops and priests political deputies either on the national or regional level so as to break the tension between Church and State and find some means of coming to terms with the Church.[18]

2. The second step was to try to win over the remaining Catholics by means of these deputies. Apparently about 80 out of the 100-plus dioceses that were asked, replied in favor of a General Assembly dealing with the affairs of the Church (pp. 23ff.).

3. The third initiative was to make certain concessions and promises such as to restore ecclesiastical properties, to found a great national seminary for the education of the clergy and to allow the publication of Catholic journals and newspapers. Faced with the constant hostility of the *ecclesiastical* hierarchy[19] the Communists even acknowledged their own errors in religious policy and their lack of knowledge of the internal work-

[15] Cf. *ibid.* p. 204.

[16] Mr. Thomas (a pseudonym) was not a member of the Peking Assembly, but was there the whole time and able to discuss the matter with important figures in the Assembly. He left China in 1959 and published eleven long articles in the *Free Pacific Magazine*. The figures here are from the 1961 volume and page numbers in parentheses refer to this.

[17] The fact that the official Communist communiqué accepted the supremacy of the pope in the dogmatic and moral fields would seem to indicate discussions in the Assembly that are unknown to me.

[18] Before accepting the post of Political Deputy of the Province of Hopei, Bishop Chao consulted Rome, but received no reply. Cf. *ibid.* p. 84.

[19] Questions such as these: Why did they imprison ecclesiastical superiors, confiscate Church property, refuse permission to visit Christians? How can this be reconciled with their protestations of religious freedom?

ings of the Church, promising to mend their ways in the future (p. 84). In this way there was a sort of dialogue—forced or not—a dialogue that was somewhat captious since the Communists always insisted on not speaking of ideology or religious beliefs but only of patriotism, of the material construction of the nation and of the well-being of the people.

The first decision (doomed to frustration) made by those who took part in the Assembly was to organize a pilgrimage to Rome to inform the Holy See of the actual situation of the Church in China and obtain mutual understanding. They then discussed whether or not two priests who had been suspended by Rome could take part in the Assembly and ended by accepting their presence (pp. 85ff.). Those whom the Communists called "right-wing" were those who defended the traditional tenets of the Church. For example, Bishop Chao Chen-sheng, S.J., of Hsien-hsien (Hopei), put the following propositions to the Assembly: to love religion is also to love one's country; following the socialist road should be voluntary, not forced; the approval of Rome would be necessary for the foundation of the Patriotic Association; the pope loves China, is anti-imperialist, a defender of world peace (pp. 136 and 206).

The matter of the election and consecration of new bishops was one of the burning questions. As the Communist proposals did not meet with the approval of the Assembly, they postponed discussion of the problem and published nothing in the press about it. The problem arose because the majority of the dioceses were lacking their ordinaries and the positions had to be filled. Some left-wingers said that since the Church in China already had its own hierarchy it should elect and consecrate new bishops as needed on its own account. But this was not accepted by the remaining participants. To find a way out, the Communists called a special session toward the end of the Assembly and invited a group of thirty of the most respected bishops and priests. They declared the results of the earlier discussion and then asked Archbishop P'i of Shen-yang (Mukden), and Bishop Chao, whether or not they would consent

to consecrate bishops chosen in this way. They both replied
that they would not, as did all the other bishops who were
asked. The Communist agents found themselves forced to admit
that it would serve no purpose to nominate bishops if these
were not consecrated. In the end, since it was an apparently
insoluble doctrinal problem and one which had in any case to
be solved by the Church itself since the government had no
views of its own, they decided to postpone a decision since no
solution could be found for the time being (p. 140).

However, one proposal made by a few priests, later accepted
by others and by the Communists themselves, marked a step
toward the solution of the problem of the election and consecration of bishops: that the Chinese hierarchy should elect
bishops and present the names for approval to the Holy See.
The candidates should, of course, be followers of the party line
but also acceptable to the Holy See. For example, the election
of a priest from Peking, who had been suspended and whom
the Communists wanted to elect, was withdrawn in face of the
protests of the priest himself, who did not want to embark on
a new quarrel with the Holy See (p. 205). The first two names
presented were bishops for Hankow and Wachang (Province of
Hopei). Rome replied with two telegrams: in the first, the
validity of the election was denied, and in the second, both
those consecrating and those consecrated were threatened with
excommunication if the consecration went forward. This was
at the end of March, 1958. This gave the Communists the satis-
faction of having predicted that Rome would react in this way,
and was a hard blow to the bishops and priests who had fought
for the names to be submitted to Rome, as they now found
themselves in a difficult situation. Those bishops who remained
faithful to the tradition of the Church remained steadfast in
refusing to consecrate, but others, including Archbishop P'i and
Bishop Chao apparently, who had previously declared: "I will
not consecrate," now showed themselves disposed to do so (pp.
206ff.). The first consecration, that of the two bishops-elect
whose names had been submitted to Rome, in fact took place

in Hankow on April 13, 1958. The consecrating bishop was
Bishop Ly Tao-nan, and he was assisted by four others. The
ceremony was performed with great solemnity and was widely
publicized (pp. 207ff.). This was followed by others in various
places so that by January, 1962, there were 42 bishops who
had been consecrated in this manner.[20]

The foundation of the Patriotic Catholic Chinese Association was, and still is, the most important event in the Church
in China. Mr. Thomas gives us a key to interpret the official
communiqués of the Communist press.[21] According to him,
the communiqué of the Second General Assembly, which took
place in Peking (January 6-18, 1962) with 256 participants,[22]
must also be taken into account. This deals with the socialist
education of Catholics, which had been started in 1958,[23] and
reaffirms the reactionary character of the Holy See; a more
positive note is perhaps struck by the repeated affirmation that
the party and the government will continue their policy of religious freedom. As for the plan for future work, the two last
points of the five put forward have a certain novelty: religious
life should be readjusted to fit the policies and laws of the government, and a theological center should be established with
the cooperation of the dioceses for the formation of the clergy
and "intellectual elements".[24] Archbishop P'i was reelected
President of the Association.

Catholics who participated in these Assemblies and in the
activities of the Patriotic Association should not be condemned
out of hand.[25] The wisdom of not passing judgment can be seen

[20] Cf. T. Hang, *op. cit.* p. 128.

[21] I met "Mr. Thomas" in Saigon in June 1963. He was convinced
that the Western world does not understand the Communist system. The
only point he would concede was that Communists did employ lying as a
technique justified in itself.

[22] For major religions there is usually a General Assembly every four
years. Cf. *China News Analysis* 439 (Sept. 28, 1962), p. 4.

[23] There is a recent account of the indoctrination process in "La persecution des catholiques chinois," in *Etudes* (Feb. 1965), pp. 264-73.

[24] These "intellectuals" would be party agents. Cf. *China News Analysis*
439, pp. 5-6.

[25] Cf. T. Hang, *op. cit.* pp. 123-4.

from the change of attitude on the part of Pope John XXIII himself. At the beginning of his pontificate he was still speaking of "the disastrous schism" [26] of the Church in China, but he never mentioned it again. His Holiness Pope Paul VI has also kept silent till now on the subject of the Church in Communist China, but in his Encyclical *Ecclesiam suam*[27] he expresses, on the one hand, his reprobation of atheistic communism, a reprobation, he says, which "is more sorrow for a victim than the sentence of a judge" (n. 105); on the other hand, he affirms: "We do not despair that they (the Communists) may one day be able to enter into a more positive dialogue with the Church than the present one which we now of necessity deplore and lament" (n. 109). These words can also naturally be applied to the present situation in Communist China. The pope's "pastoral office" above all, when he speaks of trying to "seek in the heart of the modern atheist the motives of his turmoil and denial" (n. 108), should help to create a state of mind that is, and will be, basic for a positive and constructive dialogue. The last three reasons for trying to understand the phenomenon of modern atheism which the pope gives, fit the case of China particularly well:

1. "We see these men full of yearning, prompted sometimes by passion and desire for the unattainable, but often also by great-hearted dreams of justice and progress. In such dreams noble social aims are set up in the place of the absolute and necessary God, testifying thereby to the ineradicable need for the divine source and end of all things, whose transcendence and immanence it is the task of our teaching office to reveal with patience and vision" (n. 108c).

2. "Again, we see them, sometimes with ingenuous enthusiasm, having recourse to human reason, with the intention of arriving at a scientific explanation of the universe . . . It is a procedure which leads in a direction quite contrary to the

[26] Cf. *A.A.S.* (1958), p. 985; (1959), pp. 19 and 421.
[27] *Ecclesiam suam*, nn. 105, 108, 109 (Glen Rock, N.J.: Paulist Press, 1964), pp. 60-63.

will of those who use it, thinking to find in it an answerable proof of their atheism and its own intrinsic validity, for it leads them onward toward the new and final metaphysical and logical assertion of the existence of the supreme God" (n. 108d).

3. "Sometimes, too, the atheist is spurred on by noble sentiments and by impatience with the mediocrity and self-seeking of so many contemporary social settings. He knows well how to borrow from our gospel, modes and expressions of solidarity and human compassion" (n. 108f).

The pope's establishment of the secretariat for non-believers marks a more concrete step forward. Is dialogue with the Marxists possible? The conversations organized by the Paulus-Gesellschaft in Cologne (Autumn, 1964) and in Salzburg (Spring, 1965) tried to open the way. "Communists and theologians had a chance to exchange views on their actual conception of the theme 'Man and Religion', and both sides had to admit that the thought of each was still very far from being understood by the other." [28] And with the Chinese Marxists? Nobody doubts that the Chinese Communists are true Marxist-Leninists. Since 1962 the Communist leadership has been working feverishly to form successors for the next generation. The first of the five conditions laid down by Mao Tse-tung himself is that they should be true Marxist-Leninists.[29] And if Western Marxist theorists and politicians find difficulty in reconciling their concepts of personality and personalism, democracy and liberty (Schaff) and religion (Garaudy, Bosnjak, Luporini),[30] this does not happen, or at least not noticeably with the Chinese Communists. Mao Tse-tung himself, although he is considered the greatest theorist of Chinese communism, is in fact more practical than theoretical, more of a politician than a thinker. An insignificant proportion of his enormous literary output is taken up by theoretical writings, both in quantity and quality. Marxist-Leninism is for him more a method of revolution than

[28] In *Herder Correspondence* 19 (1965), p. 417.

[29] Cf. *Tsu Kuo* ("The Homeland") 8 (Hong Kong, November, 1964), p. 303.

[30] Cf. *Herder Correspondence* 19 (1965), pp. 416-8.

a theory. He has become an idol, thanks to his undeniable qualities of vision, leadership, judgment of the whole historical situation, always ready to learn and correct himself, together with his successes in planning and in the military field, in his management of intellectuals and his achievement of giving China true independence and autonomy (even from Russia), and the whole nation is being formed by the study of his writings. But yet, how far he has moved from his earlier self with his ideal of freeing "the Chinese people from their deep and heavy calamities"! [31] Marxist-Leninism was for him the best and most effective "recipe" to free China from the imperialist yoke, and he made good use of it, although at the cost of colossal injustice and cruelty. But in the end, this recipe in his hands proved an implacable master which, instead of setting the people free, enslaved them once again in a slavery far worse than that of the previous imperialism. This is Mao's enormous crime, for which the Chinese people will not forgive him.[32] This became clear in the "hundred flowers" time of 1957; and Mao's own preoccupation with finding successors is a witness to the fact. It is also the basis of the prediction by the expert on Communist Chinese affairs, Mr. Lin Yu-ho, that the second and third generations of Chinese Communists will take the road of revisionism.[33]

The possible changes to come in Chinese communism, its basically noble concern for the good of the people, the needs and aspirations of the people themselves, are all elements that could open the way to a new dialogue. It will certainly be a difficult way, but it must come, simply because we have no alternative but to accept the reality of the situation, and the reality is, that after the first hurricane the Chinese Communists are not trying to wipe the Church out, or even to encourage a head-on clash, but they are determined to oblige everyone—

[31] Words spoken by Mao Tse-tung in 1941.
[32] Cf. Liu Lie, *The Night Will Pass* (1965), a Chinese ms. not yet published.
[33] Cf. *College Life* (in Chinese) 26 (Hong Kong, 1965), p. 9. Mr. Lin is the editor of *Tsu Kuo*.

Catholics included—to contribute to the reconstruction of their nation. For this reason, and in order to keep the door open for the future, is this the time now to think about the possibility of a dialogue and of finding a *modus vivendi*? This will naturally have to come from the top downward. For the other side to learn to distinguish between imperialism and religion does not only depend on their evolution but also on the degree to which we achieve our own reform.

Should China become an open mission field once again, the dialogue will be no less important or difficult. As Father Pedro Arrupe, the Jesuit superior general, has so rightly said, the use of the word "dialogue" in religious circles today suggests above all an attitude of mind, and if a dialogue is to take place there must be mutual respect between the partners to the dialogue.[34] A first condition for establishing a climate of mutual respect is that the partners to the dialogue should use the same language. It may be true that Communists tend to twist the meaning of words, but what effort have we made to understand what they are trying to say? Marx's saying: "Religion is the opium of the people", can serve as an example. All too often we take it as a straightforward Communist attack on religion. But if for a moment we could forget its atheistic origin surely it is rich in sociological and historical implications that should oblige us to reform or to *aggiornamento*.[35] This phenomenon of failing to fit our language to that of the other side can be found throughout the Chinese continent.[36] As for respect, those who have suffered most deserve it most; this can be applied to those who live under the Communist regime in China and equally to ourselves insofar as we try not only to preach Christ crucified but also to follow his example in our lives.

[34] Press conference at *Civilta Cattolica,* June 14, 1965.
[35] Cf. G. Cotter, O.P., "Why Communism Appeals to Developing Countries" in *Concilium,* Vol. 3 (Glen Rock, N.J.: Paulist Press, 1965), pp. 76-87.
[36] As, for example, the expressions of "martyrdom" and "shedding blood" used by the Fides Agency, which made no sense in the context of the Peking Assembly.

III

TWO TASKS: EFFECTIVENESS AND ADAPTATION

Although these two terms, effectiveness and adaptation, are not mutually exclusive but rather complementary, it is, nevertheless, often observable in missionary territories that effective people adapt less well. Therefore, these two aspects of the missionary task must be dealt with separately. We here use the term "effectiveness" in the sense of the *apostolic tasks that must be performed,* and "adaptation" as *the spirit with which they must be carried out.*

The Most Urgent Tasks

Father Ladany has proposed that the most efficacious and economic method of ensuring that the Church leads more than a marginal existence in a country where the majority of the population is not Catholic and becomes an integral part of an Asiatic nation such as China, is to win over the intellectuals.[37] The realm of ideology—philosophy, literature, social sciences, law, etc.—deserves the closest attention. Legrand and Hang both agree with this. The first considers religion and morals, philosophy, education, sociology and literature as the most important fields of influence;[38] the second asserts the need not only for systematic translation of the major works of Christianity and for intelligent and selective assimilation of Chinese culture by Christians, but also for the Church to take an active interest in the political, economic, sociological and literary activity of the country.[39] It is easy to see how disproportionate these tasks are to the personal and economic resources of the Church in China at present. This means that cooperation on the part of the intellectual Western Catholic world is essential.

[37] Cf. L. Ladany, "A Meditation on the Church in Asia, for Missionaries and Catholic Universities" in *Christ to the World* 8 (1963), pp. 244-52.
[38] Cf. F. Legrand, "The Intellectual Apostolate, Its Importance—How to Organize It," *ibid.,* pp. 195-204.
[39] Cf. T. Hang, *op. cit.* pp. 101-5.

Ladany states that if we are to win over the intellectuals, not
only are a better coordination of work and a different method
of selection and training of personnel required, but also continued support from the highest Catholic intellectual circles in
the West.[40]

One related problem is that of Chinese students abroad,
who today number more than 10,000, of whom more than half
are in the United States of America.[41] Between 1905 and 1960
Chinese students in the United States of America earned 2,789
doctorates in physics, engineering, sociology, biology, humani-
ties, etc.;[42] and during roughly the same period, 582 in France
and 755 in Germany also obtained doctorates. Counting those
in England and other European countries, and adding them
to those in America, more than 5,000 Chinese students in
Europe and America received degrees during these 55 years.[43]
And what an influence these men have had on the course of
contemporary Chinese history! The process goes on. Have
Catholic intellectuals in Europe and America reflected enough
on the responsibility of their ability to influence the course of
a nation's history? [44]

Training must, however, be deep as well as widespread, and
this requires some center of theological studies. Hang sees the
same necessity. He proposed three new sections for the Catholic Central Bureau in Taipei, of which the first would be for
the study of theology and the liturgy.[45] But how can the Church
be presented "in all its richness and all its catholicity as a reply
to the deepest aspirations of Asiatic nations today" (Ladany),

[40] Cf. L. Ladany, op. cit. pp. 251-2.
[41] Cf. Education and Culture (in Chinese) 259 (Taipei, Apr. 1961), p.
26.
[42] Cf. China Newsweek (in Chinese) 784 (Taipei, Aug. 24, 1964), pp.
3-4.
[43] Cf. Daily Central News (in Chinese) (Taipei, Oct. 17, 1964).
[44] Worth mentioning here is OFAUC (Organization for the Apostolic
Formation of Chinese Students), led by Juan Pao and his companions,
who are at present building a college for Chinese students in the University City in Madrid.
[45] The other two are for refugees and emigrants and for students abroad.
Cf. T. Hang, op. cit. pp. 210-1.

unless the Church's theology can be assimilated and thoroughly adapted to the mentality and culture of each particular nation? This task would appear to be particularly urgent in the case of China, and yet neither in Taiwan nor in Hong Kong is there a center of studies or a journal that can be called strictly theological. Many of the clergy hold degrees in philosophy and canon law, but very few in theology and Scripture. The Protestants seem to be more convinced of this need and have produced works in advance of Catholic works, such as those of the Rev. Lit-Sen Chang and Chinese translations of the works of Oscar Cullmann, E. Jacob, J. M. Kitagawa, etc.[46] This immediately brings us face to face with all the problems of seminary education, particularly theological education, problems which in the next few years are going to become very acute in relation to the problem of China.

Everyone has finally become convinced of the need for a comprehensive plan covering coordination of tasks and concentration of forces. In the last few years progress has been made in this direction. All the bishops of Taiwan together with those of Hong Kong and Macao have met frequently to discuss the problem of the Church in China above all, and to draw up plans. Since 1964, the superiors of some twenty religious orders and congregations of men in Taiwan have also held an annual reunion to explore ways in which they can better cooperate together.[47]

The Spirit of Adaptation

Just as in the supernatural order, effectiveness is not the supreme criterion, or rather in that order there is a criterion of effectiveness which is different from that obtaining in the natural order. Therefore, in missionary work effectiveness is not the whole answer to the problem of entering into contact with a different race and culture unless it is accompanied by

[46] There is a whole program in existence for this, the "Theological Text Books Program", sponsored by the Association of Theological Schools in Southeast Asia, Program Director: J. R. Fleming.

[47] Cf. *Christian Life Weekly* (in Chinese) Apr. 29, 1964, p. 4.

the spirit of adaptation. Pope Paul VI in his Encyclical *Ecclesiam suam* gives two particular indications of the directions in which a true renovation of the life of the Church is to be found which are particularly applicable to the missions. First, the spirit of poverty which, as the pope says, is that spirit which enables us to understand "so many weaknesses and failures in the past" and also shows us "what our way of life should be and what is the best way to announce the religion of Christ to souls".[48] What Bishop Kobayaski said of Japan is equally applicable to China: that the missionaries all too often live on a different level than the people.[49] This is certainly a difficult problem when it comes to putting it into practical forms, but this must not prevent the spirit of poverty from accompanying and informing all our efforts toward effectiveness. The examples left to us by Blessed Charles de Foucauld and his disciple, Father Peyriguère, should surely find more echo in far more missionaries than they do at present.

The pope's second indication is that a spirit of charity "should assume today the rightful position, *i.e.,* the first and the highest, in the scale of religious and moral values. Not only should this be in theoretical estimation, but also by being put into practice in the Christian life" (*Ecclesiam suam,* n. 58b). The practice of charity in the missions must know how to take on a local flavor suitable to the character of the people. The heart and the emotions have a very important part to play here. As long as the missionary does not lead an effective life as close as possible to that of the people among whom he lives, making their innermost aspirations his own, his charity—perhaps considered as something purely supernatural—will not be clothed in flesh but will remain abstract and sterile. But *nihil volitum quin praecognitum;* and to identify himself with the deepest feelings of the people, he must get to know them, which means studying their qualities and defects, their aptitudes and difficulties, etc.

Another book by T. Hang gives a good survey of the average

[48] *Ecclesiam suam,* n. 56a (Glen Rock, N.J.: Paulist Press, 1964).
[49] Cf. *Herd. Corresp.,* loc. cit. p. 432.

Chinese character.⁵⁰ I should like to mention some of his conclusions here. There are two central characteristics of the Chinese: his tendency toward the concrete and toward a global vision: in his affective life the chief characteristic is the remote, indirect and diluted exteriorization of his feelings. His tendency toward the concrete and the global can be seen in the whole of the history of China, particularly in the language, calligraphy and thought habits. This type of thought lacks Western logic and system, but this is not to deny it other advantages, such as agility, speed and depth of intuition, particularly in human relations. Perhaps this type of thought is closer to that of the Hebrews of biblical times. The remote expression of feelings, as can be seen for example in their painting and music, explains many manifestations often wrongly interpreted in the West as evidence of insincerity, lack of vitality, repression of feelings or even insensibility. In fact, the Chinese character corresponds more closely to what Pascal called "esprit de finesse" than to the "esprit de géometrie", which has for long periods been the dominant spirit in the Western intellectual world.

The Chinese, with their long tradition and exaltation of the ideal of moral perfection, are in many ways favorably disposed to accept Christianity, but they, like other peoples, also have particular difficulties and obstacles. In their case, the two principal obstacles in the way of their acceptance of Christianity are their inclination to relativism and syncretism and the dominance of esthetic values in their culture. Relativism and syncretism do not mix well with the dogma and intransigence of Catholicism, and excessive estheticism easily leads to laziness and loss of moral sense. The periodic decadence of the Chinese dynasties is good evidence of this. The cultivation of speculative theology such as scholastic theology, well-tempered with modern currents of Catholic theology, can help to overcome the first obstacle. To find a balanced approach to Chinese estheticism, the aspect of *pulchrum* in Christian doctrine as well as those of *verum* and

⁵⁰ T. Hang, *Grundzuge des chinesischen Volkscharakters* (1964), in particular pp. 11, 14, 31-52, 116-27.

bonum must be exploited as Hans Urs von Balthasar did in his recent book *Herrlichkeit,* and on the other hand, Christian abnegation and asceticism founded on a love of God and one's neighbor must also be demonstrated.

One of the best ways of getting to know a people is to study its history. Therefore, it is not possible to be psychologically in sympathy with the Chinese without knowing the history of the last 125 years, since the Opium War. As for the remainder of Chinese history, each period has produced its national heroes, its great writers and sages, its examples of high moral perfection held up to later generations as splendid exemplars of filial piety, conjugal fidelity, noble friendships, etc. The whole of this inheritance is a vital link among members of a nation, and the missionary must know how to make use of it to lead those he is evangelizing to God.

The Last Reflections

1. Missionary adaptation is essentially a matter of psychology and pedagogy: of knowing how to make the Gospel most easily and fully accepted. This is precisely what St. Paul says of himself: "I became all things to all men, that I might save all" (1 Cor. 9, 22). As Father Neuner has demonstrated,[51] what is called incorporative adaptation is really adaptation of revelation and dogma. This cannot be a task for everyone, but should be undertaken by some center of theological studies as I have already suggested, and by missionaries who are interested and prepared for the task. On the other hand, the spirit of adaptation which I have described applies to all. It is true that some apostolic tasks are more urgent than others, that not all missionaries have the same abilities, aptitudes and vocation; all, however, are taking an active and irreplaceable part in the overall task of evangelization. It is surely obvious, for example, that nuns working in schools and colleges, giving a good education to future

[51] Cf. J. Neuner and K. Mueller, "Akkomodation (dogmatische, missionarische)," in Lexikon für Theologie und Kirche I, pp. 240-4.

mothers of families, are performing a fundamental task for the Christian society of tomorrow.

2. In all our efforts to promote the cause of the Church in the missions we should not forget that in the final analysis, their ultimate result is a mystery. Exact calculations are useful and often necessary, but they can neither explain nor solve all the problems of the missions. One calculation that should be made is a comparison of the annual population increase of the nation with the number of baptisms and conversions, but such a calculation alone cannot explain the growth of the Church from its beginnings, let alone the life of our Lord and his holy Mother, and they, even more than St. Paul, are the models for our apostolate.[52] Of course, we should not expect miracles from God, but it is still true that the hand of God can still reach out. (cf. Is. 59, 1). He will not fail in his part. The problem is in ourselves, in our faithful and disinterested cooperation in his calling. We must be convinced that we can always go on to greater and better things, for the greatness and limitation of the human spirit and its cooperation with God consist in this. The Emperor T'ang, the founder of the Shang dynasty (18th century B.C.) had these words carved on the side of his bath:

> If you can renew yourself one day
> do it every day;
> Make your daily renewal a complete one.

[52] The discourse by Cardinal Silva Henriquez at the Marian Congress in Santo Domingo, March, 1964, is very inspiring. Cf. *Orientierung* 29 (1965), pp. 98-9.

PART II

BIBLIOGRAPHICAL
SURVEY

Marie-Joseph Le Guillou, O.P. / *Etiolles, France*

Mission as an Ecclesiological Theme

The importance of mission as an ecclesiological theme will be made clear by studying the following points: the position of ecclesiology at the beginning of the 20th century; mission and the attitude of the popes as ecclesial factors; the emergence of mission as an ecclesiological theme; and, lastly, the extension of the idea of mission.

I

ECCLESIOLOGY AT THE BEGINNING OF THE 20TH CENTURY

The Church has never forgotten that she received from Christ a mission that embodies his own mission, a mission to proclaim the Good News of salvation to men and to unite them in Jesus Christ so that one day all things may be brought under his headship. The awareness of this mission and its impact on ecclesiology were far from reaching their full effect at the beginning of this century. The bald affirmation of the Church's competence in every domain had reduced the idea of mission to a defense of ecclesiastical rights and powers.

In treatises on ecclesiology and in articles and popular works on the Church during the 19th and early 20th centuries, the idea of mission was practically absent.[1] After asserting that the

[1] On this point, see Y. Congar, "L'Ecclésiologie, de la Révolution française au Concile du Vatican, sous le signe de l'affirmation de l'au-

81

82 MARIE-JOSEPH LE GUILLOU, O.P.

Church received the mission of saving souls, nothing further was mentioned. The mission theme reappeared in a marginal way with regard to the ministers of the Church and her role in dispensing grace and the sacraments, but the term "mission" was not used because it was reserved for those distant regions where the Church was sent to evangelize. Curiously enough, the missionary movement stimulated by the great discoveries of the 16th century had scarcely any effect on ecclesiology, partly because of preoccupation with the Reformation and Counter-Reformation, and partly because of a compartmental view of the world: on the one hand, Christians and the Church, and on the other, missionary countries and pagans.[2] In short, the missionary idea did not reach the Church herself; it did not renew the different chapters of ecclesiology. Moreover, a Protestant, G. Warneck, founded the science of missiology and prompted the first great Catholic missiologists: Schmidlin and Charles.[3]

---

torité," in *L'Ecclésiologie au XIXe siècle* (Unam Sanctam 34) (Paris, 1960), pp. 77-114, and, in the same work, the articles by R. Aubert and J. Audinet. As an example one might mention *De Ecclesia Christi* by L. Brugère (Paris, 1878); this textbook for seminaries is typical, making no mention of mission. The treatise by Billot (Prati, 1909) devotes 12 pages out of 700 to the mission of the Church. More recently, S. Jáki, *Les tendances nouvelles de l'ecclésiologie* (Rome, 1957) (*Bib. Cat. Hung.* 8) includes no reference to it. There is no article in the *Dictionnaire de Théologie catholique* by Vacant and Mangenot on either the mission of the Church or ecumenism. This is all the more remarkable because these words and themes were just then becoming the object of great interest. Y. Congar, *Chrétiens désunis* (Unam Sanctam I) (Paris 1937) sets a new pattern in this regard. From the point of view of the magisterium one might compare the letter of the Argentine bishops in 1955, entitled "Les droits de l'Eglise," in *Documentation Catholique* (*Docum. Cath.*) 37 (1955), pp. 467-76, which is devoted almost entirely to the mission of the Church, with the Encyclical *Ecclesiam suam* of Paul VI, written under the influence of the dialogue with the world. In ten years a profound change has taken place.

[2] This tendency to go beyond the old notion of Christianity began with the criticism in Jacques Maritain's *Humanisme intégral* (1938) and shows itself again in the whole ecumenical movement. Cf. "Vers une théologie de l'Eglise, communion missionaire," in M.-J. Le Guillou, *Mission et Unité—les exigences de la communion* I (Paris, 1960), pp. 80-101.

[3] On this subject cf. *ibid.*, pp. 37-42. There is an important bibliographical survey being published by the periodical *Parole et Mission* beginning with its second issue in 1958 (July). Every three months it

II

MISSION: ITS REVIVAL IN ECCLESIOLOGY

Mission, first of all, has been a determining factor in the life of the Church since the end of the 18th century. During this period the Churches were confronted with *the whole world in the whole of its historical and social development*. This situation was determined by the new views of the world brought about by the general awareness of the philosophical and scientific contemporary thought of Erasmus and Galileo.

One man, Lamennais, saw in a prophetic way that the Church's missionary situation implied a complete change of pastoral methods. Unfortunately, the failure of his efforts, due as much to his own deficiencies as to the Church's spiritual immaturity, weighed heavily upon 19th-century developments and, to a certain extent, closed off theological enterprise in that century. Studies done by the Tübingen School, which might have led to a renewal of missiology by rediscovering a Christian view of history, had no material results.[4]

Gradually, however, the changes in the world affected all the Churches, and three closely linked facts, hailed by the Council as points to be investigated, revealed the new circumstances for the mission of the Church: Catholic Action, the insights of the priest-workers, and the ecumenical movement.

These three phenomena presented pastoral problems hitherto unknown and had a decisive effect on ecclesiology.

1. By these apparently insignificant activities the *whole* Church

---

publishes a bibliography of current works on the theology of mission. These bibliographies, revised and supplemented, will soon be published in book form by Editions du Cerf.

[4] L. Le Guillou, *L'évolution de la pensée religieuse de Lamennais* (Paris, 1965). M.-J. Le Guillou is likewise preparing an extensive study: *La crise théologique mennaisienne et sa signification.* With his brother he will edit a considerable amount of hitherto unpublished materials. Concerning the school of Tübingen cf. F.-X. Arnold, *Pastorale et principe d'incarnation* (Brussels, 1965), pp. 150-213. See the excellent pages in *Symbolism* by J. Moelher, 2 Vols. (London, 1843).

was affected; in spite of the small number of people involved, *the problem of the Church in the world* was brought into focus by taking new positions, by new ways of looking at things and of living.

2. This event coincided with a biblical, patristic, liturgical and theological return to sources. The rediscovery of social sciences, especially anthropology and sociology, provided, moreover, a desire and a capacity for reinterpretation and thoughtful re-structuring.

Renewed Contact with the World

The evolution of the idea of mission in ecclesiology leads us then to an examination of real life and the movements by which it expresses itself.

(a) Catholic Action was essentially the realization of *Christian man's position in the world,* expressed at first in terms of *fraternity* and *conquest,* with a collective dynamism, a boldness, a liberty that is demonstrated in the slogan: "We shall make our brothers Christian again," that is, all men. The mission of the Church was there where the laity mixed with the masses.[5]

(b) The second was the priest-worker movement. Neither this movement nor Catholic Action was a result of a missionary plan or organization, but stemmed from an encounter with men.

The experience of priests sent among the workers in Germany showed that the Church had become separated from the masses, cut off from them, and that the unbelief already detected by Catholic Action was not simply a crumbling of the lowest levels of the Church. We were in the presence of a world on the move, of an established industrial civilization that was fashioning a new man. The presence of the Church for this world, possible only by working and sharing its life, was a necessary requirement of *incarnation;* it was not a question of recovering men for the

[5] J. Comblin, *Echec de l'action catholique* (Paris, 1961); cf. C. Molette, "Brève histoire de l'action catholique," in *Lumière et Vie* XII (May-July, 1963), pp. 45-82; J. Leuwets, *Evangélisation collective* (coll. Dossiers des Masses Ouvrières) (Paris, 1964); R. Girault, *Etapes de l'Apostolat* (Paris, 1961).

Church, because the Church was not yet incarnated in these milieux. The idea of incarnating the Church was the task of the priesthood: that is, they had to become *indigenous* in order to *establish* the Church or *remake* the Church. This last expression tried to take into account the *grace of being a native,* which was clearly shown as quickly as the priest-workers became established and let it be known that the Church there would not have the same face as that with which old Christianity had presented itself. While waiting for this new appearance stemming from these priestly beginnings (in other words, growing *from within*), communion with the world appeared in a new light. The priest no longer believed that communion with the world was possible through Christian institutions, not even through the Christian community, perhaps non-existent for a long time, but rather in a *community of destiny* which paid the final price when it ended in the death of some priests in the deportation camps. From this came the idea of *detachment* from Christian structures and from a certain institutionalism in the Church.[6] And so, priests and laymen discovered that they were facing a world whose growth was already setting the conditions for the future; they placed *the Church in the state of mission.* This formula, proposed by M.-D. Chenu at a meeting in Lisieux (July, 1947), expressed the ecclesiological dimension discovered by the priest-workers.[7]

(c) The members and leaders of the ecumenical movement who suffered because of the suppression of the priest-workers

[6] The idea was already in the air. Cf. E. Poulat, *Naissance des Prêtres-ouvriers* (Religions et Sociétés) (Paris, 1961), pp. 66-156, and *Journal d'un prêtre d'après demain* (Religions et Sociétés) (Paris, 1961), pp. 66-156. For all that concerns priest-workers these two works are prime sources; additional material is found in the bibliography that he gives on pp. 15-30. Cf. below, footnote 55.

[7] M.-D. Chenu, *La Parole de Dieu II: L'Evangile dans le temps* (Coll. Cogitatio Fidei II) (Paris: Ed. du Cerf, 1964), pp. 237-42. The expression, "The Church in state of mission", is used several times by Cardinal Suhard (cf. below, footnote 52), also by Bishop Larrain of Chile at the Congress for the Apostolate of the Laity, October, 1957; the expression has been used as the title of several works: L. Suenens, *L'Eglise en état de mission* (Brüges, 1958); L. and A. Rétif, *Pour une Eglise en état de mission* (Brussels, 1965): Eng. tr.: *The Church's Mission in the World* (Paulist Press, 1964). This formula was destined to enjoy wide acceptance.

showed how much all Christians were concerned about this missionary pursuit. This was all the more easily understandable because ecumenism, along with the new situation of the Church since the early 19th century, had really originated with a missionary orientation.

The idea of mission demonstrated the urgency of seeking unity and forcefully presented the problem of the relation of the Church to the world in two ways: by aiming at "the evangelization of the world in this generation" and by encouraging, through small groups of laymen, the missions and the creation of new Churches. Likewise, ever since the International Conference of Missionary Societies in Edinburgh (1910), the missionary movement had stimulated ecumenical activity. By deciding on the merger of the International Missionary Council with the World Council of Churches, the Assembly at New Delhi (1961) proclaimed that the problem of unity could not be solved except in a missionary perspective. The shared experience of Christians in a common concern for the problems of the world was in itself a significant missionary symbol.

The true state of the missions (of the new Churches, as well as those other Churches which had become more and more aware of the *total* character of the Christian message) constrained the member-Churches of the World Council of Churches to live a more strictly catholic life: in this way it demonstrated that mission is an ecclesiological theme.[8]

Before being an ecclesiological theme, mission is a charismatic fact in the Church, an event (and at this point Vatican Council II appears in all its true dimensions) desired by John XXIII as an authentic Pentecost, which rediscovered the profound meaning of mission, of proclaiming the Gospel, the relationship of Catholics to "others" (Christians, believers and non-believers). It spontaneously rediscovered the current of the great Catholic

[8] On this whole subject, see M.-J. Le Guillou, *op. cit.;* cf. above, footnote 2. See also S. Neill, *A History of Christian Missions* (Harmondsworth, 1964), especially chapter 13, "From Mission to Church", pp. 510-77. We deliberately leave aside the evolution of Protestant thought which would demand a separate study in itself.

tradition, in the Spirit which animates it, by making the *whole* Church conscious of the enormous changes in the world.

The Attitude of the Popes and the Church

The popes have not been slow to recognize the importance of these events for the missions, even if they did find it necessary to suppress the priest-worker movement in order to study it and to allow it to mature.

The attitude of the popes since Pius XI represents a different aspect of ecclesiology that we must not overlook. The naming of the first Chinese bishops (1926) and the impetus given by Pius XI to Catholic Action in specialized groups, the attention given by Pius XII to all aspects of culture and human activity by his insistence, through the voice of the magisterium, on the Church's participation therein, the abolition of the Bull of Benedict XIV (1742) which had for 197 years been a tragic obstacle to the evangelization of China,[9] the new relations established by John XXIII with the separated Churches and even with the non-Christian world, the travels of Paul VI in search of new areas of dialogue outside the official framework of the Council itself —all these facts have contributed to revealing the true extent of the mission of the Church. But, beyond these phenomena it is even more useful to show how these same popes envisaged the impact of mission on ecclesiology.

Let us remember three affirmations of Pius XI which reinsert mission into ecclesiology: first, his unequivocal recognition of the missionary dimension of the *Christian people,* at a time when missionaries were only a priestly group selected for distant lands. "Catholic Action," he said, "does not differ from the divine mission entrusted to the Church and from its apostolate."[10] In the

[9] On May 18, 1936 (under Pius XI), the Sacred Congregation for Propagating the Faith modified for Japan the directives of the Bull of Benedict XIV (*Ex quo singulari*) which had almost entirely ruled out the local native rites and the possibility of adapting them; cf. *Sylloge praecipuorum documentorum. . . . Pontificum et S. C. Propaganda Fide* (1939), pp. 537ff.

[10] The letter *Quae Nobis,* Nov. 13, 1928, in *Docum. Cath.* (1929), cols. 390-3.

same way, he reasserts the final end of the Church, a Church for men, so as to prevent any inversion: "Men are not created for the Church, but the Church is created for men." [11] The Church is "a provisory means like all other means—her end is none other than the end of the persons who compose her and they merely find their fulfillment in her".[12]

Although it is too early to draw conclusions about the enormous work done by Pius XII, let us emphasize two salient features: a concern for keeping in touch with the whole development of modern man, especially by extending the teaching mission of the Church so as to retain her universality, and a concern for giving a hierarchical structure to this mission, for defining it and tracing its visible frontiers (this doubtlessly explains the slight attention to the theme of mission in the Encyclical *Mystici Corporis*).

John XXIII's opening *to the world* brought a more dynamic concept of the mission of the Church. In his opening speech of Vatican Council II, the two poles of his theology were evident: on the one hand, a Johannine vision in which the world is very radically divided between light and darkness, although he never identifies the two protagonists or opposes the world and the Church. On the other hand, he regards with understanding the world and its growth: it is a great achievement which the Church respects, cultivates and benefits from. Without overlooking the salvific mission of the Church, he links this to the world: "Uniting the best energies of the Church, trying to have the news of salvation more favorably received by men, it prepares somewhat . . . and shapes the path for that uniting of the human race which is basic and indispensable, so that the earthly city may resemble the heavenly city." [13] Yet, this is not a modernization or an adaptation of methods, but an effort to take into account the whole breadth of the Church's mission which prepares the way

[11] Speech given to those preaching the Lenten sermons in Rome, Feb. 28, 1927.

[12] H. de Lubac, *Méditations sur l'Eglise* (coll. Théologie 27) (Paris, 1952), p. 51. Cf. below, footnote 73.

[13] October 11, 1962; *Docum. Cath.* 59 (1962), cols. 1380 and 1384.

for the unity of the human race and, thanks to the light of Christ, gives men "an awareness of what they truly are".[14] He looks upon the Church as movement and the world as movement: two movements not opposed but recognizing each other; and so, the wrinkles must be removed from the Church so that she may draw people by force of example.[15]

Paul VI has already given the broad outline for a theology of the Church in which dialogue with the world holds an important place. Echoing the ideas of Pius XI, he affirms that the Church "is not by herself her own proper end, but her desires belong wholly to Christ, in Christ and by Christ; she is also wholly of men, among men and for men".[16]

Along the same lines he said at Milan a few months before his election: "When the Church opens herself to the world, she defines herself. . . . When the Church seeks herself, the Church seeks the world," [17] whence is derived the idea of a Church in ferment: "She detaches herself from the profane society that surrounds her and appears at the same time a vital leaven, an instrument of salvation for this world; and in this way she discovers and defines her mission." [18]

From Pius XI to Paul VI the problem of the Church's mission has been stated with increasing precision with respect to the development of the world, and has been viewed with more

[14] *Ecclesiam Christi Lumen Gentium*, "Message au monde," Sept. 11, 1962; *Docum. Cath.* 59 (1962), col. 1219.

[15] "Discours à l'Action Cath. Italienne," in *Docum. Cath.* 57 (1960), col. 1099; cf. "Discours au Coll. grec," in *Inf. Cath. Intern*, 99 (1959), p. 5. Note the decisive step taken by John XXIII (in *Pacem in Terris*) toward promoting dialogue with the world when he distinguishes between *error* and *those who err*, between *theoretical teachings* and *practical programs,* to which he adds: "It can happen, then, that meetings for the attainment of some practical end, which formerly were deemed inopportune or unproductive, might now or in the future be considered opportune and useful." See the context in *Catholic Mind* (Oct., 1963), p. 60.

[16] *L'Osservatore Romano* (*Oss. Rom.*) (Sept., 1964), pp. 14-5; *Docum. Cath.* 61 (1964), col. 1222.

[17] "Quest. Italia," (March, 1963), p. 57; this theme appears again in the Encyclical *Ecclesiam Suam*, in *Docum. Cath.* 61 (1964), cols. 1057-93. The capital importance of this text is to be stressed for all that concerns the reintegration of the theme of mission in ecclesiology.

[18] *Oss. Rom.* (Oct. 1, 1963); *Docum. Cath.* 54 (1957), cols. 1819-36.

understanding; this process in various ways gives the Church a
new bearing.

Return to the Sources: Indispensable to Ecclesiology

These factors were not sufficient to restore the full theological
meaning, even though they were of great pastoral moment. The
theme of mission is a typical example of this. In order that the
discoveries brought about in history might be seriously applied
to ecclesiology, there had to be a return to the sources.

The whole first part of this century furnished good soil both
for reflecting on events and working out a corresponding theology. A renovation of vocabulary and historical sources with
reference to the contemporary situation and teaching provided
both nourishment and a stimulus.

One can appreciate the role played by this flood of writing
of all types, in which the idea of mission, people, mystical body,
kingdom, the Word, kerygma, catechesis, witness and service
(diaconate, etc.) were restored in their biblical and patristic
context. This development brought about the reassessment of
many formulas and rigid definitions. The movement was re-
plenished at the sources. The hasty improvisations as well as a
certain dogmatism had to be modified by a better hold on tradition as a living force. In an earlier age, life and the synthesis of
its movements were better understood than now when analytical
procedures have made it more difficult and less attractive.[19]

[19] The history of the progressive reintegration of the mission theme
cannot be given here. We merely mention three types of works: (1)
Purely exegetical works that have unconsciously restored to prominence
the notion of mission from the most diverse points of view; the independence of their teaching gives to their remarks an original character.
(2) Works with a distinctly theological approach: the criticisms made by
Congar with regard to the teachings of E. Mersch on the mystical body
in *Sainte Eglise* (coll. Unam Sanctam 41) (Paris, 1963), pp. 477-8, 532ff.;
cf. pp. 467ff., as well as Congar's criticism of Malevez with regard to
the inclusion of the human race in Christ (*Ibid.*, pp. 491-2; cf. p. 483).
These are typical in the sense that a theology of the mission of the Church
underlies them. (3) Works which show the biblical foundations for contemporary themes: Y. Raguin, *Théologie missionnaire de l'Ancien Testament* (coll. La Sphère et la Croix, essays on missionary problems) (Paris,
1946); R. Schnackenburg, *L'Eglise dans le Nouveau Testament* (Unam

III

THE EMERGENCE OF MISSION IN ECCLESIOLOGY

The mutual impact of events and tradition appears in all ecclesiological thought. Its earliest usage touches upon two areas,
one ecumenical and the other socio-cultural, first in postwar
theological reflection and then in the pastoral orientation that
followed.

In his first writings between 1932 and 1937, Yves Congar
proposes three subjects for discussion in regard to Catholic
Action: the closed character of the Church which "looks from
the outside like a great and powerful organization, like a walled
city";[20] next, the need for thinking out "the possibilities and
conditions for her extension in the midst of the cultures that
surround her, for her incarnation in space and time";[21] lastly,
"the participation of laymen in the action of the hierarchy", for
which "a dogmatic justification and an ontological basis" must

Sanctam 47) (Paris, 1964): Eng. tr.: *The Church in the New Testament*
(Herder and Herder, 1965): with an important chapter devoted to the
mission of the Church, this work reveals what the Church of the New
Testament or the Church of the patristic age was according to present-
day standards with regard to vocabulary, coherence and intrinsic requirements.

[20] "Chronique de 1932," reproduced in *Sainte Eglise* (Unam Sanctam
41) (Paris, 1963), p. 449. It is to be noted that from the beginnings of
Catholic Action (1925-1954) many new periodicals whose theme of
mission was increasingly evident came into being, with more or less theological assurance depending upon the author, the year or the subject at
issue. By way of example: *La Vie Intellectuelle* (which later merged with
La Revue des Jeunes and *Les Lettres de Javisy*) for the years following
1928; *Esprit* began in 1932 but flourished especially in the years 1949-
1955; *Jeunesse de l'Eglise* has been published since 1942; cf. especially
nos. 1, 8 and 10; (cf. below, footnote 63); *Masses Ouvrières*, in 1944;
Lettre aux Communautés de la Mission de France (entitled *Unis Pour*
from 1944 to 1947), mimeographed until 1958; *Dieu Vivant* (1945-
1955); *Bulletin du Cercle S. Jean-Baptiste*, mimeographed since 1948,
printed after 1960; contemporary publications include: *Quinzaine* (1950-
1955); *Bulletin* (1955-1957); *Lettre* in 1958; *Paroisse et Liturgie*, especially in 1959; *Eglise Vivante* and *Parole et Mission* in 1958; *Testi-
monianze* (Florence) in 1957, not to mention the missionary reviews.
[21] *Revue de sciences philosophiques et théologiques* (*Rev. sc. phil. et
théol.*) 24 (1935), reproduced in *Sainte Eglise*, p. 485.

be found "in the sacramental character of confirmation".[22] All this sets up a distinction between the growing conception of a mandate and the more organic conception of the mission of the laity, which belongs to the sacramental life of the Church before being determined by an exterior act of authority.

The theme of mission reappears in three different aspects: the symbol of the Church in the world, a symbol to be transformed; her mission in life and in the diversity of cultures in which she should be embodied; the real nature of the laity, whose mission appears in a new light requiring a gradual reappraisal of the ministry.

This way of stating the problem indicates another change. It stems from the fact that theologians accept the necessity of considering unbelief as a phenomenon of conscience and even of looking at the Church with the unbeliever, not in order to refute him but to understand him. In this respect, it is quite significant that a theologian like Yves Congar has followed up the investigation of *La Vie Intellectuelle* concerning present-day reasons for unbelief with a theological conclusion.[23]

In 1937 the question of the mission of the Church was treated again in *Chrétiens désunis* (first volume of the collection *Unam Sanctam*) in a masterly way. Mission is seen as stripping catholicity of its apologetic tendencies: "The catholicity of the Church, considered as a property of her being, is the dynamic universality of her unity: her inner power of uniting, assimilating, enriching, exalting, winning to God and reuniting in him all of man, all men, and all human values." [24]

---

[22] *Rev. sc. phil. et théol.* 21 (1932), reproduced in *Sainte Eglise,* p. 463.

[23] A theological conclusion to the investigation of the reasons for contemporary lack of belief: *La Vie Intellectuelle* 37 (1935), pp. 214-49. He sees the lack of faith as a consequence of "the narrowness of the Church turned in on itself, which conspired to make Catholicism appear a part of the world, a sect, a party" (p. 249). "Neither the Church nor faith radiate in their totality upon life" (p. 247). "Our world must be filled again with signs of God": cf. 36 (June 25, 1935), pp. 357-89.

[24] *Chrétiens désunis, op. cit.* above, footnote 1, p. 117; cf. pp. 121-3 and 125. The theme of the Church's power to unite all humanity has been taken up often since then, in particular by John XXIII in his speech at the opening of the Council (cf. above, footnote 13).

Catholicity is apostolic.[25] It is essentially represented by the symbol of the Mother: "It is in the very name of this maternity which is her mission and because of the law of assumption which belongs to her that the Church has to adapt her organization to human differences." [26] The present mission has two aspects: incarnation and assumption. According to the first, it goes to men; according to the second, it gathers them up.[27] Congar develops this in a rather harsh image: the Church "gives birth within herself to children whom she conceives outside, taking them from the bosom of carnal humanity which is by nature scattered about".[28]

Here we find a patristic argument (in contrast to the thought of Teilhard de Chardin) contending that the growth of humanity is complicated by division, separation and dispersion so that men become "more and more heterogeneous".[29]

Chrétiens désunis presents an impressive ecclesiological view of mission. Future discussions and research are already forecast. Let us call attention to the principal points:

1. Mission is permanent and coextensive with the life of the Church. P. Haubtman has said: "The Church in the path traced by Congar is missionary, not by practical necessity in order to meet transitory historical circumstances, but by her essence, by

[25] *Ibid.,* p. 125.

[26] *Ibid.,* p. 128. Concerning this adaptation: "The Church which participates inwardly with the infinite nature of the divine being will always be expected to participate in the infinity of human development" (p. 131); cf. pp. 133-48.

[27] Cf. B. Besret, "Incarnation ou Eschatologie; contribution à l'histoire du vocabulaire religieux contemporain (1935-55)," in *Rencontres* 66 (1964), pp. 90-1. He violently opposes the way Congar unites the themes. The same balance appears in E. Suhard, *Growth or Decline* (Notre Dame, Ind.: Fides Publishers, 1947); M.-D. Chenu, *op. cit.* above, footnote 1 *passim;* cf. H. Fries in *L'Eglise et Tradition* (Le Puy, 1963), pp. 253ff.

[28] P. 129. Congar will be faithful to this theology of the mission linked to the symbol of maternity; the same theme is found in the preface of the book by K. Delahaye, *Ecclesia Mater chez les Pères des trois premiers siècles* (Unam Sanctam 46) (Paris, 1964).

[29] *Chrétiens désunis,* pp. 126-8. In this book the theme of mission comes to the support of ecumenism (which is the principal object of the volume) and Catholic Action (which occupies pp. 131-7) without limiting itself to the West.

her very way of living. The mission exists everywhere, in countries referred to as missions as well as in Catholic countries." [30]
With this in mind, M.-D. Chenu used the phrase, "the Church
in the state of mission",[31] but H. Godin and Y. Daniel were
emphasizing at the same time that the mission is something very
precise and quite distinct from a parish, even one that is reno-
vated and renewed in its apostolate.[32] On the premises of Y.
Congar, the distinction between the missions and the mission of
the whole Church remained open. On the other hand, once the
mission was understood as the life of the Spirit in the Church,
there still remained the whole problem of the relation of the
new missionary impulse to Church structures and of charism to
the institution.

2. By linking the mission of the Church to the incarnation of
Christ and by explaining this mission in terms of incarnation,
Congar was able to reiterate a traditional theme, developed so
lucidly by J. A. Mohler: "The Church then is Jesus Christ always renewing himself, reappearing in human form: *she is the
permanent incarnation of the Son of God.*" [33] In spite of its balanced perspective, this theme, henceforth linked to the mission
in theology as well as in human experience, met with obstacles:
distinctions were soon made between incarnation and eschatology, humanism and the supernatural, human development and
sacrifice, etc., as is shown by B. Besret in his book *Incarnation
ou Eschatologie.*[34]

3. Congar had already shown the historical import of the mission of the Church, but his historical dimension had not yet the

[30] *Semaine religieuse de Paris* (Oct. 26, 1963), p. 1031.
[31] Cf. above, footnote 7.
[32] *France, Pays de Mission* (Coll. Rencontres 12) (Paris, 1943); quoted
according to the 1962 edition: Coll. Le Monde 26, p. 46.
[33] *La symbolique, op. cit.* above, footnote 4, pp. 6-7. This text was extensively used by Cardinal Suhard in *Growth or Decline* (Notre Dame,
Ind.: Fides Publishers, 1947).
[34] *Op. cit.* above, footnote 27, pp. 23-105; cf. pp. 169ff. This presentation is limited and incomplete (cf. pp. 12-3 of the preface by Chenu.)
Congar keeps developing this theme: "The Church is the continuation of
the incarnation in history." *Chrétiens en dialogue* (Unam Sanctam 50), p.
430 and *passim*.

amplitude that it would have in his later works. In *Chrétiens désunis,* the grasp of the amplitude of the world and of the development of cultures does not let us know what status is to be given to creation or to the progress of men and humanity; in other words, does humanity flow from within the Church, a distinct society including the unity of all, or will the Church, scattered throughout this world, have her full flowering in Jesus Christ at the end of time? In summary, we have the Congar tendency and the Teilhard tendency which will be taken up with regard to mission in very famous debates.[35]

In 1937 the subject of mission was taken up in a broader view that was synthetic, but controversial by reason of the rapid development of events, the progress of theology and their divergent tendencies. These must be analyzed now through the mind of M.-D. Chenu who, more than anyone else, determined their course.

Catholic Action and the Modern World

The starting point for M.-D. Chenu is not the missionary situation as such but a sociological one and the analysis of their mutual relations; he saw the Church "in the state of mission" at the point where the Gospel affects the world in its process of development.

Chenu reveals the dimensions of the mission of the Church, that is, of its historical setting:[36] industrialization and its repercussions on work, the phenomenon of socialization, the political and economic order. This immense expansion of society and man sets the stage where the mission of the Church and the faith are worked out.[37] It seems that mission does not differ from faith

[35] One must be careful not to harden these divergent tendencies in their opposition; in each author they should be restated from a wider viewpoint, a view less clear-cut, more subtle and never completely delineated.

[36] Chenu remarks that on several occasions he borrows in part Jacques Maritain's analysis in *Humanisme intégral* (Paris, 1936), ch. 6.

[37] *La Parole de Dieu II: L'Evangile dans le temps,* pp. 87-107. With Congar they confine themselves to those writings prior to 1940, trying to understand how the theme of mission was rediscovered during those years along with the rise of Catholic Action among the workers.

in its relation to the world, in the free play of divine life on the whole of mankind. Mission is the realm of faith lived in the world, a faith that interprets events and that "looks at all things with the eye of God",[38] but also an incarnate faith that takes responsibility for the growth of humanity so that it becomes "the communitarian growth of the grace of God, in Christ".[39] By means of this faith that looks at the world, Chenu restores the mission of the working man and the journalist, and at the same time restores that of the theologian; they are no longer "on the border of separate domains" but "facing the same reality".[40]

And thus all is reunified, reconciled: the Christian mission of the working man is no longer a side issue in his life; his brotherly love is no longer "like a pious corrective, sweetening the harsh blow of an economic structure previously established, a sort of lubricant assuring the smooth meshing of wheels set in motion with no concern for man";[41] the fraternity that he establishes requires, on the contrary, those structures and those associations that the economist, the sociologist and the politician observe and, in order to bring them about, it aims at permeating social functions and values in their own right and in their most autonomous requirements.[42]

The journalist "is involved" more than anyone else "in the anguish and hopes of humanity—seeing there the basis for divine life";[43] "he is truly and by profession the hero of evangelical liberty".[44] The theologian rediscovers his mission, since theology, like every act of faith, puts one in dialogue and in a state of mission. He finds the inspiration that restores the spiritual armor and organic power of faith, because his thought develops in contemporary milieux and intellectual circles, and because he finds there that easy spontaneity in "the most strenuous encoun-

[38] *Ibid.*, p. 223.
[39] *Ibid.*, p. 489.
[40] *Ibid.*, p. 217.
[41] *Ibid.*, p. 488.
[42] *Ibid.*, p. 481.
[43] *Ibid.*, p. 223.
[44] *Ibid.*, p. 224.

ters with philosophies and cultures, that constant creation in the midst of the most highly developed organisms . . . and that holy boldness in the reasonable joy of the light of faith".[45]

From that time on the writings of Chenu point prophetically to the essential elements of mission:

1. The Church's mission is not considered solely from the point of view of its internal dynamism. It manifests all that the world in its activity and real attainments teaches the Church with regard to her mission. One is not tempted to think of the Church as an accumulation of power which takes over the remnants of a world incapable of unity. The maternal image used by Congar does not take into account the Church's whole mission; that of the leaven inserted in the dough is indispensable.

2. The theology of incarnation is vigorously developed in a missionary direction. "Some misunderstand and go counter to the basic impetus of God's plan. Christ does not save man by carrying him off with him to heavenly regions, but by putting on himself, God, the state of humanity." [46] This does not mean that Christ does not lead to the Father, but that he does so by way of the incarnation.

Following a tradition that goes back to St. John, Chenu holds that Christ returned to his Father at the very moment when he was incorporating himself into the human condition until death, linking himself to all who would be recapitulated in him, and not only afterward as an extrinsic recompense for his actions.[47] The incarnation is not finished at Christmas, just as the redemption did not begin in Gethsemani. The entire incarnation is a sacrifice which makes Christ's mission coextensive and involved with humanity, and not a localized task.

3. Mission finds itself integrated with the whole web of history,

[45] Ibid., p. 260. One might mention here the importance of a short work: Une Ecole de Théologie: Le Saulchoir (Paris, 1937), in which Chenu develops the theology-mission relation; a chapter was reprinted in La Parole de Dieu I: La foi dans l'intelligence (cf. above, footnote 7), pp. 258ff.; cf. on the same subject La Parole de Dieu II: L'Evangile dans le temps (1936), pp. 271-4; (1938), pp. 216-24; and often repeated.

[46] L'Evangile dans le temps, p. 482.

[47] Ibid., p. 219 and passim.

with all creation, so that mission itself becomes once again a source of life for those who consecrate themselves to it. Theology itself belongs to this mission because "the difficult task of viewing and judging each day the events of the world in a Christian way can be accomplished only by a faith that is founded on theological knowledge".[48]

4. Thereafter, Chenu approaches the question of the institution and the mission by trying to understand the role of Catholic Action with regard to the parish. It took courage because relations were very tense. Since the parish could not penetrate society, he thought that Catholic Action should be recognized as the appropriate means. However, the problem of their relations persisted.

In a period when scarcely any reexamination of Christian institutions was allowed, and when these institutions were more or less on the margins of society, he rediscovered with an extraordinary independence a program of life dominated by a faith in close relation with all observable reality.

Missionary Institutions

Between the cry uttered in *France, Pays de Mission* (1943) and the opening of the Council (1962), a profound awareness of the mission of the Church was widely effected. *France, Pays de Mission* presents a striking picture of a universe from which the Church is absent. Impressed by their Jocist experience, H. Godin and Y. Daniel called for a new world where "the gestures of Christ who is made man and comes to the earth to save us" must be renewed. The word "mission" indicates this "sending" of truth and light to individuals and societies that are deprived of it.[49]

The purpose of this sending is specified: "*A missionary goes to the place where as yet there is nothing:* he is sent to establish the Church of Christ in this kind of human community." [50] The

---

[48] *La foi dans l'intelligence,* p. 260.
[49] *Op. cit.* above, footnote 32, p. 18.
[50] *Ibid.,* p. 18. The idea is developed throughout the book explaining

whole book tends to bring out the original character of mission which brings the Church to birth when parishes, fixed, closed, disarmed in the face of modern paganism, have not this vital power. In short, by this initial insight the field of the mission was opened, but "those who answer this calling are distinct from the rest of the Church already established and caught up in administration". The distinctive aspect of mission is forcefully asserted. The distinction goes as far as the bishop who "cannot be considered a missionary, but rather a pastor. He is going to govern a flock, obviously joining concern for conquest to concern for good administration".[51] This statement will not of course be acceptable in a theology of mission.

For years after the appearance of *France, Pays de Mission,* Lisieux was one of the centers for reflection on mission. Cardinal Suhard had set up there the Seminary for the Mission of France. The necessity for leaving the ghetto, for forging new ties with the world, was affirmed. "In order that the mission be accomplished . . . there must be priests who are above all concerned with this immense problem facing the Church: there must be an integration of its message with the civilization that is being built . . . [and] priests capable of seeing all the aspects of the larger problem and capable of finding a solution that is a missionary action." [52] These are the "actions that the Church must perform" while preserving a concern for the whole, what Congar will call

the type of relation to the world that mission specifies: the work is a collective testimony rather than a sociological or a theological work.

[51] *Ibid.,* p. 18.

[52] L. Augros, "Conclusions de la session," in *Lettre aux Communautés de la mission de France* (December, 1948), p. 2. One would wish that the writings of L. Augros (superior of the Mission de France from 1941 to 1952) were gathered in one volume, for the conclusions of sessions and other articles in *La Lettre aux Communautés* or in *Masses ouvrières* (1948) are texts too precious to be summed up, and they are almost inaccessible in mimeographed form. At the same time attention is called to the writings of Cardinal E. Suhard. One whole volume of selected texts has been published by O. de la Brosse: *Cardinal E. Suhard: Vers une Eglise en état de mission* (Coll. Chrétiens de tous les temps) (Paris, 1964). The substance of his work is represented by his last three pastorals: *Growth or Decline* (1947); *Meaning of God* (1948); *Priests among Men* (1949), which together form a triptych of missiology. (All three works published by Fides Publishers, Notre Dame, Indiana.)

agere ut pars.[53] "There is a need for men, priests and laity, who agree to leave the Christian sociological universe to plunge into the completely pagan universe and bring to birth the Church there like the missionaries who leave for Africa." [54]

This breaking away involves certain features that are brought up in the priestly discussions at Lisieux: "abandonment of privileges and social advantages" in order to be "with the poor in their life of work"; "to plunge into poverty" (impossible in the parish); "separation from territorial ties in order to join world movements and especially the worker movement"; "freedom from the obsession with worship in the interests of life"; "separation from bourgeois culture" in order to enter into "a common destiny" with the world and "to feel with the poor"; "independence of organizational structures".[55]

These disavowals represent the Church's fidelity to her mission with an evangelical determination to transform all things in a double communion of the Church and the world.

"This *reformatio* (thanks to which the Church will be faithful to her mission) will not be effected by an ecclesiastical decree (authority, canonical decision, etc.), or by political paths (tactics, diplomacy, new organizations), or by economic and social transformation, or simply by presence in the world, incarnation, openness and communion with all that has value (even theological value) in the world today, but by the adoption of a complex attitude *which conciliates or unites the return to the sources and presence in the world*. Return to the sources first, return to the Gospel—communion in faith with the living tradition of the Church understood in all its breadth and all its power of growth, its dynamism, its biological riches which, by wedding the world,

[53] Y. Congar, *Jalons pour une théologie du laicat* (Unam Sanctam 23) (Paris, 1952), pp. 481ff.: Eng. tr.: *Lay People in the Church* (Newman, 1965); cf. *Vraie et Fausse Réforme dans l'Eglise* (Unam Sanctam 20) (Paris, 1950), pp. 271-491.

[54] L. Augros, "Editorial pour le 10ème anniversaire de la fondation de la Mission de France," in *Lettre aux Communautés . . . (1951-1952)* 1 (November 14, 1951), p. 6.

[55] "Session de la Mission de France" (discussing the priesthood), in *Lettre aux Communautés . . .* (October, 1950).

make us capable of carrying out in its values a work of discrimination, elimination and assimilation that will find fulfillment in creating an indigenous Church." [56]

L. Augros thereupon insists that this effort is "made as a Church by the collaboration of all in the Church" and of each one in his place.

Certain characteristic elements of mission must now be clearly evident: (1) breaking away is only one form of being sent into the world; (2) it is worthwhile only if a deeper communion begins to be formed in one's life and consciousness; (3) by this sending, the Church begins to live the Gospel in the world and the Church discovers the world; (4) communion presupposes an entrance "from below, in a purely evangelical way, by being stripped of everything".

Development of Missionary Institutions

This type of breaking away had to provoke wide discussion. Was it not contrary to the catholicity of the Church and the Christian priesthood to let priests install themselves in a social class? Bishop Ancel wrote in 1951 to the priest-workers: "A priest . . . has not the right to belong to a social category." [57] "The Son of God did not agree to take on any particular social category, but human nature as a whole. . . . A priest has no more right to become a worker than a member of the bourgeoisie . . . although certain things require a study of bourgeois culture in order to save [it]." [58]

[56] L. Augros, "Conclusions de la Mission de France, September, 1950," in *Lettre aux Communautés* . . . (October, 1950), pp. 17-8. The Church is still "wholly engaged in this effort" (parishes, laymen). An Anglican priest-worker, J. Rowe, explains this in a striking way in *Priests and Workers, a Rejoinder* (London, 1965): "In fact, what the priest-workers insist on is simply to take their own part in the mission with respect to the working classes. They are not asking the Church for a movement of worker priests . . . that is why from the beginning laymen have formed part of the group" (p. 33; cf. also p. 36). Rowe's book is in response to the remarks of Bishop Wickham in a book whose title Rowe has borrowed: *Priests and Workers: an Anglo-French Discussion* (London, 1961).

[57] *Cinq ans chez les ouvriers—Témoignages et réflexions* (Coll. Le poids du jour) (Paris: Centurion, 1963), p. 65.

[58] *Ibid.*, p. 53.

This remark brings us to a more discerning analysis of solidarities as prime determinants of the mission and its situation.
Men of the Church and the Church herself cannot avoid involvement in events with social implications. Chenu analyzed and
described economic solidarity and ties of every sort throughout
the past. He showed how every evangelical awakening challenged
existing solidarities.[59]

Mission was still basically directed toward proclaiming the
Good News and evangelization, and the conditions of this were
limited by the possibilities of encounter. But the hope of a new
Christianity born outside the parish was disappearing; it faced
the Church with the two immediate requirements of mission:
first, liberty for the spokesman, the autonomy which is necessary
for a human encounter to be true and for a conversation with
God to be possible; secondly, the need for the whole Church to
be transformed as a function of the mission.

Y. de Montcheuil had insisted, even before the war, that the
apostolate presupposed "a liberty which, in its complete self-
possession, gives itself in love".[60] Following John XXIII, one
can say: "Every human being has a right to liberty in the pursuit
of truth." [61]

The development of the mission went further; it showed that
even human encounters with all men require respect for this
liberty: "An encounter is not truly human unless the partners,
thanks to the autonomy of their procedure, are free, including
the elimination of a paternalism necessary no doubt in former
times." [62]

This liberty is not simply a respect for being, for life, for
conscience, as one respects a growing plant; it involves reciprocity

[59] L'Evangile dans le temps, pp. 50-3, 153-4, 434-5, 479-85, etc. St.
Thomas d'Aquin et la théologie (Coll. Maîtres spirituels 17) (Paris,
1959), pp. 6-17 (cf. Toward Understanding St. Thomas [Regnery, 1964]),
shows how the poverty of the mendicant orders dissociated them from
the oppressive economic order and changed the patterns of social solidarity. Even those who are not aware of it belong to a social class.
[60] Y. de Montcheuil, Problèmes de vie spirituelle (Paris, 1957), p. 33.
[61] Pacem in terris (Glen Rock, N.J.: Paulist Press, 1963).
[62] M.-D. Chenu, L'Evangile dans le temps, p. 262.

among the spokesmen or the partners of an encounter or dialogue; it is internal law for the growth of a society which agrees to go beyond heterogeneous juxtaposition and to involve itself deliberately in an organic effort toward unity in which all are transformed. The encounter really implies reciprocal transformation on the part of the one who brings the mission of Christ into this world as well as of those who receive him.

According to this point of view, encounter presupposes complete disinterestedness, to the point of not trying to convert people. Fr. de Montcheuil, keenly aware of the human value of going to God freely, emphasizes "the absurdity of any purely intellectual effort". The point is not to persuade or convince, but "to awaken to a new life. . . . We are not in the realm of proving anything, but of communicating values".[63]

P. A. Liégé speaks of this problem more extensively while emphasizing the collective aspects: "The struggle of a Christian

---

[63] Y. de Montcheuil, *op. cit.*, p. 35; cf. pp. 32-5 and *Eglise et Monde actuel* (Paris, 1959). The expression "not to try to convert them" does not imply an agreement with the thesis attributed to M. Montuclard, *Les évènements de la foi* (Jeunesse de l'Eglise) (Paris, 1951), which was criticized by L. Suenens, *L'Eglise en état de mission* (see footnote 52), and also by J. Montini, *La Mission de l'Eglise* (cf. above, footnotes 7 and 18); according to this thesis, two phases are distinguished: first, humanization or human liberation, and then evangelization, which would be excluded from the first phase. It seems, however, that Montuclard, realizing that evangelization is not feasible in certain social structures, and that a Christian or priestly life will not succeed in awakening faith (cf. Charles de Foucauld), is convinced that it is advisable to involve oneself in the unbelieving milieux and remain resigned to one's ineffectiveness; but, because he did not emphasize that this involvement must be a sign that the Good News is already reached by an unselfish life, serious misunderstandings resulted and falsified his point of view. On this subject there are enlightening remarks in H. Perrin, *Journal d'un prêtre-ouvrier en Allemagne* (Paris, 1945), pp. 53-4; T. Rowe, *Priests and the Workers*, p. 31. The idea of a pre-mission in the work of L. and A. Rétif (*op. cit.* above, footnote 56), p. 129, and already mentioned by Peyriguère, gives an acceptable form to the stages required by Montuclard. Between the establishment of evangelizing signs and the formation of faith (which it is our business to improve) there comes conversion which belongs to God and goes beyond our powers. That providential disposition (according to which we can mediate in the work of conversion only under mysterious conditions arranged by God) opens a perspective wider than that of one individual trying to convert another.

community toward liberty has a necessary missionary significance
. . . in that the Church appears as the place of true liberty . . .
the place of brotherly respect." [64] As H. de Lubac said, she
"secures liberty for men" and "the spread of the testament of
liberty".[65]

This liberty proves to be a phenomenon within society. Its
conditions are not confined to the negative and restraining elements by which religious pressures are removed; liberty refers to
situations, to cases of conscience where human and religious aspects are inextricably blended in a specific historical context. One
is led to envisage a freedom of societies. "This dialogue of the
Church with the modern world implies in this regard unequivocal
positions. . . . It calls for involvement on the part of Catholics,
which means that they recognize a pluralist world." [66]

The Church no longer on the defensive would thereby show
that no one can be denied his essential liberty: his liberty to show
forth our God and Father in Jesus Christ, whose passion and
death were not obstacles that could deprive him of the liberty
to exercise his mission, but were instead the supreme moment for
the sign of salvation.

Freedom in encounter brings us to the second condition for

---

[64] P. Liégé, "La liberté religieuse, impératif de la Mission," in *Parole
et Mission* 27 (1964), p. 538. In the pamphlet (out-of-print), *Journées
missionaires de la Tourette* (Economie et Humanisme) (February,
1947), A. de Pierre said: "The object of the mission is that a given
human group should mount toward Christ of itself, that it should radiate
the spirit of Christ. The members of this group should be brought to
take complete responsibility for themselves, by themselves, etc." (p. 53).
This marks an important advance in recognizing the problems of a confrontation of the Church with the world, problems that still are to be
solved.

[65] H. de Lubac, *Méditations sur L'Eglise* (Coll. Théologie 27) (Paris,
1952), pp. 129-36. The expression *Testament de la liberté* is borrowed
from St. Irenaeus.

[66] P. Liégé, *op. cit.*, p. 546; see also his presentation of the book by
G. de Broglie in *Parole et Mission* 27 (1964) where two restrictions are
laid down to be carefully observed for clear thinking about the mission
of the Church: (1) respect for the consciences of those who do not share
our faith and who may be led toward truth by paths that elude us; (2) a
less positive appreciation of Christianity out of concern for openness toward dialogue.

mission: the requirement regarding the means put at its disposal. This requirement is far-reaching because it lays down the condition for the Church's action, determines her image in the eyes of men as well as her coherence with the testimony of those whom she sends.

When those sent give up their goods and positions and modify the interplay of solidarities, they risk cutting themselves off from ecclesiastical society, if the latter is rigid. Such is the consequence of the double communion set up by the basic activity of the mission.

In fact, when people have seen that the Gospel and those who proclaim it "had no external show by which to impress and attract attention" [67] and that the Church holds to keeping this, there is a scandal of division bearing some analogy to the schisms: one side does not recognize the mission of the other.[68] The non-believer tends to dissociate the man of the mission from his Church so that he may be free from any danger of compromise. Moreover, Christianity is in danger of no longer recognizing the mission, and he who is not recognized also does not recognize, in those who resist him, the Gospel that he lives.

Consequently, the mission insists, in the name of the Gospel that it has been sent to live and the mission that it has received from the Church, on a return of the whole body to the Gospel. Such a request requires structural reforms. In fact, the whole institutional setup is called into question.

This problem, often raised before,[69] is very complex because

[67] L. de Conninck, "Les conversations de Dachau," in *Nouvelle Revue Théologique* (1945), pp. 1169-83; cf. E. Poulat, *Naissance des prêtres-ouvriers* (1965), p. 234. The solidarities that affect the missions involve some risks; cf. A. Laurentin, *op. cit.* below, footnote 77.

[68] L. Augros, "Le prêtre et les crises de la foi," in *Lettre aux Communautés . . .* (1951-52), no. 2, p. 39; J. Frisque, "Les contestations de la mission," in *Lettre aux Communautés . . .* (November, 1960), pp. 3-13, reprinted in *La Revue Nouvelle* (February 15, 1961) and in the *Lettre* (March-April, 1961) no. 34, with a subsequent exchange of remarks in nos. 35 and 37.

[69] "If there is a unanimous agreement among theologians about the fact that the Church as a whole is charged with the mission (footnotes 7 and 56), that the Church as a whole is always and everywhere a witness . . . by its existence . . . not by the activity of a few." Cf. Y. de

mingled with the evangelical question are two different ways of acting: one proper to institutions, the other to mission.[70] Let us take a parish, for instance. Like any institution, it creates and defines its space, or place of encounter. It grows by assimilating elements, but it does not assimilate by adapting itself. Structures are not assimilated; they are transformed. The parish is not the leaven that can be thrown, as it were, into the world, as can those individuals who belong specifically to the mission. Moreover, its proper mission is not first of all to be sent to those at a distance, but to make the journey toward the eucharist. Consequently, it has perhaps been a mistake to try to "articulate" everything around the parish and similar institutions. The episcopacy, we shall see, is in another order: it is the mission in essence, collegially at least, contrary to the affirmation of Godin.[71]

It is still true that, among the diverse movements and institutions, it is the same Gospel and the mission of the same Lord, as well as the same Church by which we live. It is also certain that when "sensitivity to the Gospel is renewed and, as it were, sharpened by a return to its inspiration, its freshness and its first thrilling impulse", the weight of institutions will have to be shaken off so that "a return to the letter of the Gospel" may be possible beyond the institutions.[72]

The tensions and conflicts which result are in many respects

Montcheuil, *Problèmes de vie spirituelle* 44. "The Church as a whole mediates for the world . . . the Church exercising a total ministry." Cf. Y. Congar in *Ministères et Laïcat* (Taizé, 1964), p. 139; it remains nonetheless true that the relating of life to institutions presents more problems when life and relation to the world display a wider range of activity. *Jeunesse de l'Eglise*, no. 8: *"Je bâtirai mon Eglise,"* stated the problem in a pointed manner. It was approached from various points of view (not, however, opposing a Church of law to a Church of life, an institutional Church, to a Church of charity); for example: "Charisms and Functions," in Y. Congar, *Vraie et fausse réforme; Jalons;* M.-D. Chenu, "Mission et chrétienté"; Y. de Montcheuil, "Evangile vécu et formalisme," *op. cit.,* p. 33 and pp. 51-2; J. Frisque, "Régime sacral, régime profane" (cf. footnote 129; P. Liégé, cf. footnote 70).

[70] P. Liégé, "La mission contre les institutions chrétiennes," in *Parole et Mission* 15 (October, 1961), pp. 495ff.

[71] Cf. above, footnotes 32, 49, pp. 8, 12.

[72] M.-D. Chenu, *L'Evangile dans le temps*, pp. 30ff.; cf. *idem*, St. Thomas . . . , *op. cit.* above, footnote 59, pp. 7-17.

(rather than human weaknesses) a sign of the profound life of faith in the Church, which spurs on its fidelity and renews its witness by a purifying trial.

Under various forms, the Church is put in a position to live the mystery of Christ without the required means altering the mystery, her manifestation in the poor and in the Church. "In reality," said Chenu at Lisieux, "it is the Church that is under the obligation of defining her mission, not from without . . . but from within, in the aspirations of our faith." [73]

Something like this is found in the basic book by G. Mercier, bishop of Laghouat and M.-J. Le Guillou: a study of the mystery of poverty. "What can one say," writes Bishop Mercier, "if the Church herself in her bishops and priests has not succeeded in stripping herself of what remains of her pomp and temporal power, of reliance on human means, in order to return to the essential directive and to the most striking sign of the divine mission of her divine pastor: 'The poor have the Gospel preached to them' " (Luke 7, 22; cf. 4, 18ff.; Is. 61, 1-2, and *passim*);[74] and he goes on: "One is obliged to see in the Church as a whole a lack of contact with the poor that is a real scandal. . . . The Church no longer gives the sign that she is truly the Church of Christ." [75]

[73] "Les dépassements de l'Eglise d'après les leçons de l'histoire," in *Lettre aux Communautés* . . . (October, 1950), pp. 2ff. Inversely, there is the "incurable discontent" that the Church provokes in the world by her Gospel: H. de Lubac, *Méditations sur l'Eglise*, pp. 136ff.; cf. *Splendour of the Church* (Glen Rock, N.J.: Paulist Press, 1963); Y. de Montcheuil, *op. cit.*, pp. 37, 42, 44, 48.

[74] *Mission et Pauvreté, l'heure de la mission mondiale* (Coll. l'Eglise en son temps) (Paris, 1964), p. 35; cf. Y. Congar, *Pour une Eglise servante et pauvre* (Coll. l'Eglise aux cent visages) (Paris, 1963), and the works of P. Gauthier.

[75] *Ibid.*, p. 33. The idea of a split (hence, moat, walls) is very pronounced in Cardinal Suhard's works; cf. O. de la Brosse, *op. cit.* above, footnote 52, p. 298 and *passim*, linking Romans 9, 3, and Ephesians 2, 14; this is the critical point with regard to "the real impossibility for the Church of becoming indigenous". Cf. A. Henry, *Esquisse d'une théologie de la mission* (Coll. Foi vivante) (Paris, 1959), p. 14. This leads certain people to reverse the statement: "The workers have left the Church" to "Christianity has left the workers", implying that it is her responsibility to make herself present.

But the Church as a whole does not go to the poor without revising her whole life and she does not revise everything without going to the poor. The reason for this is given by Le Guillou, who shows the relation of poverty to the very structure of the mission and not merely as a particular activity, a structure at once diachronic and synchronic with the mission of the Church. Poverty is an "ontological condition of the life of the Church, bringing into play her original strength";[76] love of the poor is "the visible sign" of the mission and the "institutional framework of the Church".[77]

This book does not suggest a scientific investigation in order to understand poverty better; it proposes the restoration of those signs by an encounter with the poor.[78] Without, however, neglecting the sociological view of the situation, it does not call for the creation of benevolent institutions to which official recognition would be granted and which would be integrated sacramentally as functions of the diaconate.[79] Here the concern is for the way in which the Church will accept ties that impoverish her: it is a phenomenon of conversion that goes far beyond a few detachments.

Consequently, Le Guillou is led to envisage the mission of the Church as the condition whereby the Word receives its value as a sign among the poor. That is where it finds its catholic character and shows its sacramental nature.

Linked with the sign, the Word becomes an act of communion;[80] the evangelical Word is heard if it leaps over the wall of

[76] M.-D. Chenu, *L'Evangile dans le temps*, p. 126.

[77] *Ibid.*, pp. 59-60; cf. pp. 183-4. The expression "institutional structure" of course supposes here that the structure is *organic* and not architectural; on this subject cf. A. Laurentin, "La place du risque dans le christianisme," in *Esprit* 33 (1965), pp. 145-50.

[78] M.-J. Le Guillou, *ibid.*, pp. 111-7. Moreover, sociology knows nothing about the poor who are not a group, a class or a social category, but an evangelical category, while remaining a tangible reality.

[79] Y. Congar, "Ministère et laïcat . . . dans la théologie catholique," in *Ministères et Laïcat* (Semaine Roman de Théologie pastorale) (Taizé, 1964), pp. 128-31, scarcely seems to correspond with the theological and pastoral requirements for an authentic sacramentality and a true mission.

[80] *Ibid.*, pp. 109-95. The connection between mission and signs is brought out with force by A. Souques, "Le signe de l'humanité de Dieu

abstraction that separates us from men, and it forms a sign of friendship which is also a sign of love of God and of the power of the Spirit. The priesthood is consecrated to the Word; it is the guarantee of its efficacy. It is in order to give sacraments to men that the priesthood is a sacrament, but it is also to be a bridge by which the Church overcomes the incomprehension that surrounds and holds her. In one person all the gap between unbelief and the final banquet is bridged.[81] Through the priest, Word and sacrament are one, and, as St. Thomas says: "The place of sacrifice is the same as the place of preaching." And so, the restoration of the Word implies the restoration of the priesthood in a world where men sometimes feel "closer to a Chinaman than to a parish priest".[82]

If he identifies himself with the poor, it is not a mere peculiarity which cuts him off from the rich: it is by reason of that "fundamental law of the apostolate: catholicity in poverty". And Le Guillou adds: "Except for persecution, perhaps . . . the most authentic sign of participation in poverty and in the authentic human condition on the whole is work." [83] In short, mission and poverty go hand in hand.

Mission and the Internal Life of the Church

Mission considered as an encounter with the world and as a phenomenon of evangelization was to have immediate and profound repercussions on questions touching the Church. It is

---

aujourd'hui," in *Lettre aux Communautés* . . . (November, 1963). This view of things does not take into account another problem stated in *Jeunesse de l'Eglise* 1 (1942), p. 24, which is still a great difficulty in the theology of the mission: namely, the adaptation of ends proper to the activity of the Church and those that are proper to temporal activity; this question underlies the debate caused by the work of Teilhard de Chardin. It cannot be considered within the limits of this survey in spite of its importance.

[81] M.-J. Le Guillou, *op. cit.* above, footnote 74, p. 110.

[82] *Ibid.*, p. 142. M.-J. Le Guillou had already pointed out the difficulties that "particularly involve missionary activity" with regard to the "missionary structure of the Church", including the relations of priesthood to laity, pp. 91-108.

[83] *Ibid.*, p. 115; cf. pp. 114-7. See also J. Rowe, *op. cit.*, pp. 36ff., who sees a sort of incompatibility between mission and any sort of *leadership*.

important to trace this, briefly traversing three domains: the path that goes from conversion to the eucharist, the organic ministry of the Church and catechesis.

Mission was to bring about a better knowledge of the steps leading from the call of God to the sacraments. Mission brought to light the distance which separates one from the other, the time needed for covering this distance and the profound connection between them, conferring on the whole procedure a sacramental value.[84] It has also caused the restoration of catechesis.

"Mission precedes the catechumenate; it gives it its style," writes F. Coudreau.[85] At the moment when Christians present a catechumen, they testify that God has "always been at work in their life": they call for "respect for the world from which the catechumen comes". "The catechumenate is not only the entrance of a man into the Church; when a man is baptized, the world is baptized, a civilization, and, in the world so constructed, the kingdom of God." [86]

This sequence of events leads to an unavoidable criticism of the hasty application of the sacraments that is very widespread throughout Christendom. The hesitation of certain priests with regard to the administration of the sacraments, almost unheard of now, seems profoundly meaningful for the mission of the Church in the light of the theology concerning faith in its relation to sacrament.[87] At the present time this is the main source of renewal in ordinary pastoral activities.

This presupposes an enlarged view of the responsibilities of the clergy and their capacity for initiative. Therefore, it is not

[84] A. Henry, *Mission Theology* (Fides, 1962); A. Laurentin and M. Dujarier, *Recherches historiques et pastorales sur les étapes catéchuménales* (Brüges, 1965); A. Laurentin, "Lettre d'un prêtre à son évêque," in *Paroisse et Liturgie* (April 1, 1963), pp. 201-17.
[85] "Le catéchuménat du diocèse de Paris," in *Paroisse et Liturgie* (May 15, 1964), p. 394.
[86] *Ibid.*, p. 395. Cf. F. Coudreau, *Semaine Religieuse de Paris* (March 23, 1963), pp. 269-86; (March 30), pp. 301-20; and *Problèmes de Catéchuménat* (supplement to the review *Catéchèse*) (Paris, 1962).
[87] A. Laurentin, "Bulletin bibliographique sur le problème 'Foi et Sacrement'", in *Foi et Sacrement* (Coll. de Past. Lit. 62) (Brüges, 1964).

astonishing that certain questions are earnestly asked concerning the possibility of linking obedience to these vitally conceived common responsibilities of the priesthood, rather than to the application of rules and decrees.[88]

A new awareness of this obligation appears linked with re-vitalizing the parish by making a connection with the mission and refusing to accept the division of parish/mission established by H. Godin. G. Michonneau's book, *Revolution in a City Parish,* was a direct reply, yet Cardinal Suhard in his preface does not give his unqualified approval.[89]

On the other hand, the connection of mission with the liturgical revival gave a new value to "the dynamism of the assembly". T. Maertens emphasizes moreover that it is not only the assembly which is called into question but also the celebrants "inasmuch as the assembly sees in its president the minister of worship rather than a missionary, and the essential meaning of the assembly—the sign of universal fellowship—is thoroughly blurred".[90]

Looking at the conditions of celebration at the time of the apostles, he concludes: "Those who are charged with the relation of the Church to the world preside over the assembly." [91]

Along the same lines J.-M. Gille considers that "it is in the eucharistic heart of the missionary priest that, from the moment his mission begins, the grace indigenous in the world to be evangelized—in which he becomes a sharer when he receives the mission—meets the whole of the Church".[92] This in no way aims

---

[88] A. Turck, "Le problème de la loi—Réflexions pastorales," in *Paroisse et Liturgie* (Jan. 1, 1965), pp. 3-13; cf. E. Marcus, *ibid.,* pp. 36-49. On the same subject, cf. J. Gille, "Sur les contestations de la mission," in *La Lettre* 35 (May, 1961), pp. 15-8; 37 (July, 1961), pp. 26-36.

[89] *Collection Rencontres* (Paris, 1948); Eng. tr.: *Revolution in a City Parish* (Westminster, Md.: Newman Press, 1950).

[90] T. Maertens, *L'Assemblée chrétienne—De la Théologie biblique à la pastorale du XXe siècle* (Coll. de Past. Lit. 64) (Brüges), p. 75; cf. pp. 41, 47, 49-58, 71, 73, 94, 101-3. This is the first time that so much attention has been given to the impact of mission on the assembly and the celebrant; many passages concern the bishop, in whom T. Maertens theologically and biblically establishes the unity mission (eucharist) without denying the difficulties in its realization.

[91] *Ibid.,* p. 71.

[92] *La Lettre* 37 (July, 1961), *op. cit.* above, footnote 88.

at making the eucharist a means of converting non-Christians, but at showing the sacramental structure of the missionary act which, by right, "pours forth from the heart of the eucharist".

The question of the parish, as a depository of the eucharist, claiming the mission, is the subject of a still incomplete study.[93] The challenge of the second quarter of this century has not yet been taken up.

One reason behind the problem of the parish derives from the fact that the ordering of functions in the Church, their mutual relations and their relations with the world has been reexamined [94] in the laity, in the diaconate, in the priesthood and in the episcopacy. Studies concerning the laity must emphasize the role of the charisms in the Church as a manifestation of the Spirit inherent in the mission. In the *Constitution on the Church*, the theme of mission, the central thread, recognized the vital role of that prophetic spirit which animates pastors and the faithful, but it stresses rightly that "the responsibility for proclaiming the Gospel everywhere on earth pertains to the body of shepherds", that is, the bishops[95] united with the priesthood.

[93] C. Floristán, *La paroisse, communauté eucharistique* (Coll. Théologie, recherches synthèses XIII) (Paris, 1963); *Paroisse et Liturgie* (special issue, Aug. 15, 1963); K. Rahner, "Réflexions sur les principes constitutionnels de l'Eglise," in *L'Episcopat* (Unam Sanctum 39) (Paris, 1962). Except for A. Turck (*Paroisse et Liturgie*, special issue) there is a tendency to make the parish absolute, in the sense that it unites mission and eucharist. At the present time it has been perceived that the opportunities for openness and vitality in a parish presuppose the acceptance of a mission, Catholic Action and a catechumenate (which are distinct from it, but with which it collaborates vitally). Such a collaboration finds its unity in the eucharist of the bishop: A. Aubry, *Inf. Cath. Int.* 243 (1965), pp. 3-4.

[94] As a result of the work of Y. Congar and especially of the Council, studies are being multiplied, but it does not always seem that the functions and charisms are understood practically in the mission of the Church. Cf. the stimulating book by J. Barreau and D. Barbe, *Le Prêtre dans la Mission* (Paris, 1965) which shows precisely where mission as an ecclesiological theme again raises the question of the situation of the priest, his dealings with the laity and ecclesiastical structures.

[95] N. 23, edited by P. Camelot (Unam Sanctum 51) (Paris, 1965), p. 59. The missionary function corresponds with the character of the People of God whom they serve (nn. 16-17, pp. 41-5). Consequently, the faithful are animated by the Spirit according to different graces, in order that the

Mission, finding its unity in a theology of the Word, was to play an important part in the whole working out of catechesis and the attention given to a revival of the notion of kerygma.[96] It is not only children's catechisms and preaching to adults that were thereby affected, but the whole proclaiming of the Christian message and the most advanced levels of teaching, for it has become clear, on the one hand, that the Word of the Church must adapt itself to the level of faith, and, on the other hand, that it cannot develop except in permanent contact with the human universe in the culture and history where we find ourselves.[97] The uniting of the Word with the act was the key to one's missionary relevance. It is inherent in the very Word of God.

IV

THE EXTENSION OF THE IDEA OF MISSION

As a consequence of all these renewals, the idea of mission was challenged. Ohm, Seumois and Vögele recognized around 1950 that no definition of the concept of mission enjoyed the unanimous acceptance of missiologists.[98] Only one thing was clear: the notion of mission, as Warneck had presented it and as it was used by great missiologists like Smidlin and Charles, was clearly inadequate. These men thought they had to define mission

---

mission of the entire people be made manifest (n. 12, p. 35; n. 39, p. 102; n. 91, pp. 105-7; cf. also pp. 107-11). Cf. J. Sauvage, "Les dimensions missionnaires du presbyterat," in *Vocation* 228 (1964), pp. 485-96.

[96] A. Rétif, *Foi au Christ et mission* (Coll. Foi Vivante) (Paris, 1953); A. Henry, *Mission Theology* (Fides, 1962). The kerygma, a synthetic emergence of the Good News in full life, is necessarily a form of the Christian message which has the savor of mission and which requires the most adaptation; cf. *Bulletin du Cercle St. Jean-Baptiste,* nn. 1-2 (1960); n. 6 (1961), etc.

[97] The problems of catechesis and of pastoral theology came out of the missionary movement. Until the Council, the word *catechesis* does not appear in dictionaries except under its philological aspect. The review *Catéchèse* was founded in October, 1960.

[98] With regard to the thought of Ohm, J. Thauren, A. Seumois, Vögele, O'Connor, Lefebvre, etc., see E. Loffeld, *Le problème cardinal de la missiologie et des missions catholiques* (Rheims, 1956), pp. 6-7.

as *plantatio Ecclesiae,* understood especially in an institutional sense. This doctrine had certainly received some approval in pontifical teaching (Benedict XV, Pius XI and especially Pius XII in *Evangelii praecones*),[99] but it ran the risk of being interpreted in a purely juridical way, in immediate dependence on the positive law of the Church, without sufficient theological perspective. Mission was "an activity proper to the ecclesiastical ministry whose special function can be determined only by the authority of the Church and *therefore* in a positive, juridical manner".[100]

To tell the truth, the principal flaw found in Charles' position was that there was not a sufficiently strong link with the institutional Church and with the sign of the Spirit which is the ecclesial community, and that he considered it to be the *institutional Church* which, *after* her erection, gives the signs. The Church is not a sign *afterward,* but she must be and remain true to her real sign-giving nature while she is in the process of development. Charles' view depends in fact on an idea of the Church deriving from Bellarmine, which is certainly not false but incomplete.[101] Its thesis, which makes the implantation of the Church the specific missionary work, needed to be inserted into a broader missionary *theology.* De Menasce contributed to this basic evolution on a missiological plane.[102] He replied to P. Charles and A.

[99] Benedict XV, Pius XI and especially Pius XII in *Evangelii praecones, A.A.S.* (1951), p. 507.

[100] A. Seumois, *Vers une définition de l'activité missionnaire* (Beckenried, 1952), p. 19. Cf. E. Loffeld, *op. cit.,* p. 28. On the thought of A. Seumois, cf. his *Introduction à la théologie des missions* (Rome, 1961).

[101] See on this subject N. Dunas, "Perspectives d'une théologie missionnaire—Missions extérieures et missions intérieures," in *Parole et Mission* (Oct. 3, 1958), pp. 342-66; "Complexité de la Mission," in *Parole et Mission* (July 2, 1958), pp. 188-200, and P. Liégé, "La Mission comme 'plantation de l'Eglise,' " in *Conclusions du colloque de Parole et Mission* (Feb. 28, 1959); *Missions sans frontières* (Paris, 1960), pp. 249-63. See also E. Loffeld, *op. cit.,* pp. 26-7.

[102] The articles by P.-J. de Menasce are, unfortunately, scattered in *L'Annuaire Missionnaire Catholique de la Suisse* (Fribourg): "Catholicité de l'Eglise et ordre de la charité" (1939), p. 8; "Islam et universalisme" (1940-1941), p. 8; "Apostolat civilisateur et colonisation chrétienne—Considérations rétrospectives sur les réductions du Paraguay" (1942), p. 68; "Du rôle des laïcs en pays de mission" (1943), p. 8; "Les missions

Perbal (who thought they had to attack the theological thesis of the priority of charity and attribute to missions a formal motive distinct from that demanded by the entire activity of the Church) that the whole Church was missionary: "There is among all Christians endowed with grace an ordering more or less explicit toward the missionary intention of the Church, which has the same extension as the salvific will of Christ." [103]

Moreover, he emphasized that the underlying basis for implanting the Church was superabundant, lively faith, the condition required for the apostle to be capable of facing the "resistance of the most difficult audience".[104] Similar expressions are found in a recent book by F. Loew, *Comme s'il voyait l'invisible*.[105]

This deepening of our doctrine finds its completion in a work by a friend of de Menasce, C. Journet.[106] In 1964, A. Rétif wrote: "In Journet, one can say that missiology receives its scientific consecration and enters fully into theology, and more precisely into ecclesiology." [107]

---

et l'après-guerre" (1944), p. 6. In *Acta Tropica* (Bâle): "La doctrine sociale catholique et les missions d'Afrique" (1945), p. 193. In *La Nouvelle Revue de Science missionnaire* (Beckenried): "Polarité de l'activité missionnaire" (1945), p. 81; "La théologie (protestante) de la mission selon M. Kraemer" (1945), p. 241; "Une voix de la jeune Afrique" (1946), p. 161; "Sur le nationalisme des pays de mission" (1947), p. 1; cf. "Permanence et transformations de la Mission," in *Spiritus* 21, pp. 400-10. A forthcoming book entitled *Permanence et transformations de la Mission* (Paris, 1966) will collect all these essays.

[103] P.-J. de Menasce, "Catholicite," *op. cit.*, p. 13 (above, footnote 102). The position of P. Charles is found in *Les dossiers de l'action missionnaire* (Louvain, 1939), and that of A. Perbal in *Premières leçons de théologie missionnaire* (Paris, 1937). See also P. Charles, *Missiologie. Etudes, Rapports, Conferences* (Louvain, 1939).

[104] P.-J. de Menasce, "Polarité," *op. cit.* above, footnote 102, pp. 82-3.

[105] J. Loew, *Comme s'il voyait l'invisible* (Paris, 1963). The role played by J. Loew in the worker mission is well known; see his *Journal de la mission Ouvrière* (Paris).

[106] C. Journet, *L'Eglise du Verbe incarné II: Sa structure interne et son unité catholique* (Paris, 1951), pp. 1223-53. See also the very fine essay of L.-M. Duvailly, *Envoyés du Père—Mission et apostolicité* (Paris, 1960).

[107] A. Rétif, "Trinité et Missions," in *Eglise vivante* 6 (1954), p. 18. H. de Lubac had already written some beautiful pages on this subject in *Catholicisme* (Paris, 1936).

This also was the period when A. Chavasse in *Eglise et apostolat* brought mission into the very heart of ecclesiology. He showed that God, even in the Old Testament, is presented as wanting to be the pastor of a flock which he really loves and for which he wants to provide all the means of making this love efficacious. The mediator, he in whom and by whom the plan of the supreme pastor takes on a body, presented himself as the shepherd of a flock for which he is at the same time an active recruiter, the shepherd who guides and keeps them alive, and the sheepfold which welcomes them within itself and reassembles in its unity the scattered children of God. From this double aspect, the ecclesial organism must be shown as prolonging, either instrumentally or vicariously, this double function of Christ, since she is the instrument of Christ who recruits with power and the social and sacramental place for gathering his adopted sons. The Church seems like an ordained troupe of pastors who go out to men in order to unite in God the whole flock of God, and who also gather around their brethren those whom God has called through their help.[108]

In a desire for ecumenical service, Le Guillou took up a similar idea when he defined mission as: "The impetus which takes the Church of Jerusalem to the extremities of the earth, from Pentecost to the Parousia, by a process of assimilation and integration of all that in one way or another is foreign to her, even opposed to her; or else that impetus which leads her to Christianize what does not belong to her or what belongs to her only imperfectly. Moreover, it is in this missionary process of assimilation that the Church is always finding herself more and more; she becomes more aware of her own tradition and gradually makes more explicit her various aspects." [109] He showed that the mission of the Church, in the face of an unbelieving, Marxist world, religiously divided (and even more divided as Christians, but seeking unity), appeared in all its catholicity, inseparable from

[108] A. Chavasse, H. Denis, J. Frisque, R. Garnier, *Eglise et apostolat* (Paris/Tournai), 1954.

[109] M.-J. Le Guillou, *Mission et Unité—Les exigences de la Communion* II (Paris, 1960), p. 13.

ecumenism by reason of the interdependence of all the preceding elements. Ecumenical work lived on a call to the plenitude of catholicity, conceived not as a fact but as a task to be accomplished, as an internal obligation to construct and reconstruct continually the signs of its universality in one communion becoming more and more manifest. One basic principle dominated his study: Mission is the supreme regulative principle of all ecclesial activity.

As Fr. Congar said: "The Church understands what it is to be catholic by becoming so. . . . She will know what it really means for the Gospel to be preached to every creature only when that is done." [110]

More and more distinctly, the thought of Le Guillou was formulated in the thought of mystery, in the Pauline sense of the word. He saw in this the basis of mission and unity in their mutual relations: "Only that conception of mystery puts the Church in a fully theological perspective: it can thus be seen in the ensemble of God's plan, as well as in its pastoral and missionary dynamism, centered around the cross and the eucharist, all tending toward eschatology." [111]

In this ecclesiological view of mission admirably set forth by J. Dournes in his two books, *Dieu aime les païens* (Paris, 1963) and especially *Le Père m'a envoyé* (Paris, 1965), missions, as described by many missiologists, are defined as efforts to convert the unbelieving world to faith in Jesus Christ.

Ohm, for instance, distinguishes the following elements: (1) the sending of messengers of the Christian faith to non-Christians; (2) the action that corresponds to this sending and which consists of "making disciples of Christ", "making Christians", that is to say, Christianization (of men and non-Christian peoples) striven for or accomplished by those sent by God; (3) the result

[110] Y. Congar, *Esquisses du Mystère de l'Eglise* (Paris, 1941), pp. 126-7.

[111] M.-J. Le Guillou, *Le Christ et l'Eglise—Théologie du mystère* (Paris, 1963), p. 15. See also "Le fondement ecclésiologique de la mission et de l'unité," in *Unité des chrétiens et conversion du monde* (Paris, 1962), and "L'Eglise et le mystère," in *Le Mystère d'unité II: L'Eglise en plénitude* (Paris, 1962), pp. 11-53.

of this action, the men and peoples who have become disciples.

The "sending" to those who from a religious point of view are far away or outside, and not the "sending" to distant lands or to foreign peoples, is what defines mission according to the words of John XXIII: mission aims at "those peoples who are not thoroughly enlightened by the light of the Gospel".[112]

"Plantatio Ecclesiae" or Proclamation of the Word

The *plantatio Ecclesiae* (the more traditional term) certainly represents an important objective of mission, but it would be false to define it by that term alone. Ohm emphasizes that the New Testament, the Fathers, the popes and the Sacred Congregation for Propagating the Faith, even when they referred especially to setting up new Churches, never defined mission as the implanting of Churches, but as the *proclaiming* of salvation which is the communication of life.[113] Along with A. Rétif, we can see that "mission is the work of preaching everywhere until finally the Church is established".[114]

Let us try now to itemize certain points reviewed in recent research.

Basis for Mission

The rediscovery of a dynamic vision of the People of God involved in history and the Pauline notion of mystery show clearly that the basis for mission is the trinitarian mystery.

Mission comes from the Father, the infinite first principle,

[112] T. Ohm, *Faites des disciples de toutes les nations* I (Paris, 1964), pp. 51-2. The quotation from John XXIII is in *Principes Pastoraux: A.A.S.* 51 (1959), p. 834.

[113] T. Ohm, *ibid.*, p. 50. See also K. Muller, "Praedicate Evangelium, idée centrale des encycliques papales missionnaires," in *Zeitschr. für Missionswiss. und Rel. wissensch.* 44 (1959), pp. 161-73.

[114] A. Rétif, *Introduction à la doctrine pontificale des missions* (Paris, 1963). On this subject, see "Repenser la Mission," in 35 *Semaine de Missiologie de Louvain 1965* (Paris-Tournai, 1965). The talk by Yves Congar, "La Mission dans la théologie de l'Eglise," (pp. 53-78), strongly emphasizes the deficiencies of a poorly founded theology of *plantatio Ecclesiae* and makes a vigorous plea for the integration of mission and ecclesiology. See also M.-J. Le Guillou, "La vocation missionnaire de l'Eglise," a commentary on n. 17 of the *Constitution on the Church,* in volume 6 of G. Barauna, *L'Eglise de Vatican II* (Paris, 1966).

origin of all procession and of all divine mission, and it returns to him. It is expressed in the Son, the source (by his redemptive and transfiguring incarnation) of a visible and social realization of salvation, the Church. It is accomplished by an incarnation, the assuming of humanity in order to save it, in that way so well known to the Greek Fathers; in short, by "being with"—and the notion of mystery makes it very clear that poverty is theologically woven into the fabric of mission.

The mission of the Spirit is there, so that by means of the Church, sent as a whole by Christ, by means of the apostolic ministry and the sacraments, there may be effected in all what was effected once in one single being for all men, as Congar showed so well in his article, "Apostolicité", in the encyclopedia *Catholicisme*.[115]

In other words, the objective of the Church is, through the co-operation of all her members, to call the people to faith in God and in his plan of salvation by Jesus Christ in the Church, in the mandate given to the apostles and to their successors, by *proclaiming the Good News of the Gospel*; and so, she is to be made fully present to men, so that they participate fully in the mystery of Christ. Mission consists, therefore, in an expansive movement which will be accomplished by attaining the fullness (*plērōma*) restored by Christ to his Father, which comes from the Father and returns to the Father.[116] All could be summarized in a formula dear to the Greek Fathers: "From the Father, by the Son, in the Holy Spirit—in the Holy Spirit by the Son, back to the Father." [117]

The Eschatological and Crucified State of the Church

Thanks to the invisible mission of the divine persons, creation which came forth from God is constantly returning to God. To

[115] Y. Congar, "Apostolicité" in *Catholicisme*.

[116] On this subject see the work of C. Journet, *op. cit.*; that of H. de Lubac, *Le fondement théologique des missions* (Paris, 1946); the well-known work of J. Daniélou and A. Rétif, *La Mission—Eléments de théologie et de spiritualité missionnaire* (Paris, 1963); G. Mercier and M.-J. Le Guillou, *Mission et pauvreté* (Paris, 1964); C. Couturier, *Mission de l'Eglise* (Paris, 1957).

[117] C. Journet, *op. cit.*, p. 374.

state the problem in these terms is to show that the mission of the Church is situated in that tension between what she is in Jesus Christ and what she is in this world. By measuring each day the distance that separates what the body of Christ really is and what she should be, the Church becomes aware of the depth of the missionary calling.

In his book, *Sendung und Gnade,* Karl Rahner showed perfectly that the missionary nature of the Church, by a necessity inherent in salvation history, called for a situation of universal diaspora. To think that the place taken by the Church in public life in the Middle Ages is linked to her essence is to forget that she is by her very nature a sign of contradiction.[118]

"In fact, we see that the beginnings of schism and the de-christianization of the West through the Reformation and the Renaissance and the Enlightenment do in fact appear at just that moment when, on a substratum of European expansion, the Church begins to be in actuality a worldwide Church. In the moment when she begins to be a Church of *all* the heathen, she also begins, everywhere, to be a Church *among the heathen.* The actual combination of these events is, of course, loaded with guilt and tragedy; but, seeing it at the higher level of theology, and of a theology of history, it is nevertheless included with a mysterious 'must', something that should not be a surprise or a scandal to a believing Christian, because it was in fact to be expected, as indeed he has to expect the continuance of guilt and of rejection of Christ even to the end of time." [119]

---

[118] K. Rahner, *Sendung und Gnade.* French tr.: *Mission et Grâce* (Paris, 1962); cf. Eng. tr. *The Christian Commitment* (New York: Sheed and Ward, 1964). H. Urs von Balthasar, making a rapid summary of the development of the Church since the end of the Middle Ages, writes: "Many people today are ready to give their life for the Church and the world (and not at all for their own perfection). They need a theology which views Christian life as service, mission and participation in the source of energy where the Church attains completion. If a theology clearly thought out along these lines could be achieved and also popularized by its adoption into Christian teaching, Christian communities could radiate this new force over the world." Cf. "Raser les bastions," in *Dieu Vivant* 25 (1953), p. 32.

[119] K. Rahner, *op. cit.,* pp. 30-1.

In this way Rahner finds the theological basis for all concrete modern Christian attitudes:

"The Church is becoming everywhere a Church of the diaspora, a Church which lives in the midst of a multitude of non-Christians, a Church consequently embedded in a cultural, civic, political, scientific, economic, artistic context which is not the work of Christians only. This is a necessity inherent in salvation history, allowing the Church to calmly draw some conclusions as practical rules for our pastoral work; this is true whether it concerns conquest or defense, the hierarchy of the Church or the simple faithful. These conclusions set up a dialectical opposition to the obligatory rule according to which Christianity must be spread and defended, according to which it must seek by all possible means to win to Christ all men and all the special divisions of culture. It is this dialectical unity, formed by opposing maxims, which forms the charter defining the position of the Christian in the world today." [120]

This analysis implies that faith in the modern world need not be protected by sociological barriers, but exposed, developing resistance in the intimate and profound conviction of whence it comes, and in prayer on which it relies. Faith must be continually thought of as a task, and with a keen awareness of its radical simplicity.[121] Moreover, it must be lived in a pluralistic world where cultural values are not specifically Christian, where one's conscience is tested by direct opposition to Christian ethical stands.[122] In other words, the Church in diaspora becomes a Church with active members, a Church of laymen who feel genuinely responsible as individuals: the laity receive obligations

[120] *Ibid.*, pp. 33-4.

[121] *Ibid.*, p. 34. See also K. Rahner, "La foi du prêtre aujourd'hui," in *Katholikentag de Hanovre* (1962); see *Evangéliser* 101 (1963), pp. 463-91.

[122] *Idem, Sendung und Gnade (Mission et grâce*, pp. 34-35). The turning point is undoubtedly the 18th century. This remark of Perouas is to be noted: "Only the working out of a genuine Christian anthropology could have given to this period (1694-1724) its thoroughly human dimension and allowed the Church to assimilate the developments of the 18th century." Cf. *Le diocèse de la Rochelle de 1648 à 1724* (Paris, 1964). Cf. *Sociologie et Pastorale*, p. 409.

which they take up in a responsible way for the good of the Church, but also with rights similar to those enjoyed in the primitive Church; they are not people who must think themselves honored to be able to do something for the hierarchical Church and for the clergy.[123]

Consequently, the Church in diaspora will have a more religious and more interior-looking face than ever before and her clergy will no longer automatically have their place among the socially privileged. "To be a member of the clergy remains a status in the Church, but [this status] will not always be, to the extent that it has been, a status in secular society." [124]

In a general way *Church and State* will no longer be like partners face to face, struggling against each other or regulating their relations by concordat. Such a situation belongs to the past; it existed because the whole world (or very nearly the whole world) was rooted both in the State and in the Church. In the future, relations between Church and State will derive from individual lives and will depend on the conscience of each one. The State indeed is no longer the government exactly, or a monarch, but the people itself (not generally Christian), and this has nothing to do with the form that the organization of the State takes: the patriarchal type of State is in any case a thing of the past. Now the people are for the most part indifferent to the Christian interests of a portion of the population and the Church is no longer an organization whose power could be exercised widely and directly on the political level.[125]

Perhaps we should underline in this respect the importance for the contemporary world of contemplative communities, which are an eschatological icon of the Church.

The most contemplative view of the Church, and therefore the one most aware of the importance of the poor, is also the most missionary in the last analysis. This has been shown forcefully by the experiences of Fr. de Foucauld and Fr. Voillaume of the Little Brothers and the Little Sisters, and by Fr. Peyriguère, Fr.

---

[123] *Mission et grâce,* pp. 36-7.
[124] *Ibid.,* pp. 37-8.
[125] *Ibid.,* p. 38.

Ploussard, Fr. Monchanin, Fr. Le Saux, Fr. Deleury, Fathers Francis Mahieu and Bede Griffith. It is paradoxical to realize that for the modern world these are the most eloquent models of missionary action. We do not think that there has been any loss here of the meaning of the Word, but rather an acute perception that mission presupposes *such a radical* transparency that it requires the transformation of the whole being to be a witness of the *mirabilia Dei* and to be available for encounter with the *other*. These men testify to the fact that the first act of mission, insertion into the world of the poor to share their life, is entirely one with the eucharist which introduces us to the experience of the trinitarian mystery. It is the "moving and painful mystery of the sccd cast on the earth", in the words of Fr. Peyriguère.[126]

Fr. Monchanin reminds us forcefully that India will open wide its mind and heart to the paschal message of Christ on "the day when the Church appears at last as what she essentially is: an adorer prostrate at the feet of the most high God, silently withdrawn into the heart of the one in whom she makes her dwelling".[127] Fr. Le Saux's book is an illuminating document revealing how a man living in the heart of India can find again by himself the tradition of the first centuries of the Church: mission and tradition here find again their full value.[128] Here, too, it becomes

[126] We shall merely recall a few names. See Peyriguère, *Laissez-vous saisir par le Christ* (Paris, 1962); *idem, Le temps de Nazareth* (Paris, 1964); J. Ploussard, *Carnet de route* (Paris, 1964). This contemplative intention is not lacking in the minds of the priest-workers, as J. Hollande writes: "These priests wished to be above all, as Father Godin desired, contemplatives plunged into action." Cf. "La mission de Paris," in *La Christianisation du prolétariat* (Brussels-Charleroi, 1948). A. Depierre adds: "More than men of action, we are contemplatives," in *Journées missionnaires de la Tourette* (ed. Economie et Humanisme) (February, 1947), p. 52. Fr. Gauthier, a priest-worker in Nazareth, asserts: "An authentic contemplative vocation is essentially missionary," in *Les mains que voici* (Coll. Chrétienté nouvelle) (Paris, 1964), p. 174; many passages of the book reinforce this statement. The underlying connection between work and contemplation is emphasized by Charles du Foucauld, and one can find texts with the same intent in Cardinal Suhard and H. Godin.

[127] J. Monchanin and H. Le Saux, *Ermites du Saccidânanda* (Paris: Casterman, 1956).

[128] H. Le Saux, *Sagesse hindoue et mystique chrétienne du Vedanta à la Trinité* (Paris, 1965). On this whole question cf. R. Panikkar, "In-

clear how important this missionary vision is for the very structure of the contemplative life: it calls for a profound commitment in the patience necessary for impressing deeply the mystery of Christ on men and on cultures by poverty.

It is urgent that monastic life be put in the true perspective of the total mission of the Church: more than ever monks need to live, at the very heart of the Church, that kind of life which by its very self is a sign of the presence of God in the world of the poor.

Definition of Mission

We have already faced the problem of defining mission. We should like to go a little deeper into this study by following the thought of J. Frisque and J. Laloux because of its sociological dimension. It is close to the anthropological presentation of Chenu, and it corresponds by and large with the analyses by Le Guillou of the divisions preventing the integration of civilizations that differ culturally.

Frisque's definition, borrowed by Laloux, is: "Mission is the continual effort that the Church makes to convert the non-Christian world to faith in Jesus Christ. It goes to men where they are in their socio-cultural milieu. For this reason, it assumes new forms, it finds, the specialists say, new ways of acculturation, drawing upon the rich treasure accumulated in the course of its history and reread in the light of Scripture, and it lies in wait for the 'initial' grace which is at work in the non-Christian world, and which normally fructifies in the Church." [129]

---

tégration de la pensée de l'Inde," in *Bulletin du Cercle S. Jean-Baptiste* (February, 1963), pp. 16-22.

[129] J. Frisque, "Pour une théologie des rapports entre la mission et la paroisse," in *La Revue Nouvelle* 35 (1962), p. 519. See the list of articles by J. Frisque which deserve to be assembled in a volume: "La théologie de l'Eglise," in *La Revue Nouvelle* 15/11 (1959), pp. 513-26; "L'esprit missionnaire," in *Bulletin de liaison de l'ACMESS* (November, 1960); "Comment l'Eglise peut-elle rassembler des peuples différents?" in *Terre entière* 5 (1964), pp. 74-86; "La paix du Christ. Visage de l'Eglise et rythmes du monde," in *Chrétiens dans l'Univers* (Ouvr. Coll.) (Paris: Casterman, 1964), pp. 165-87; "La tentation du Christ, de l'Eglise et du chrétien," in *Assemblées du Seigneur* (Coll.), n. 26, pp. 91-102; "La pauvreté qui fait vivre," in *Paroisse et Liturgie* 15/11 (1961), pp. 529-40; "Pour une théologie de la mission," in *La Revue Nouvelle* 15/10 (1960),

Frisque says that "to evangelize is to set up the sign of the resurrection by starting with the historical roots of the mystery of Christ at the very heart of the spiritual destiny of a people".[130] Mission implies along with the proclaiming of the risen Christ a "pre-evangelization which Christians accomplish by helping to found the terrestrial city, giving their faith in the risen Christ and their participation in the ecclesial community as a visible sign of the salvation received from Jesus Christ. Pre-evangelization and evangelization are two aspects of one and the same missionary activity".[131]

With these matters clarified, let us analyze the sociological mechanism of mission, which presupposes an explanation of the sociological notions of *institution* and *culture*, transferable to another level as elements in the theological notion of mission.

J. Laloux gives the following definition of *institution*: "a combination of behavior patterns and activities performed in a fairly stable and permanent way by men in society, and organized in roles and well-structured relations in order to pursue a com-

---

pp. 257-69; "La mission dans l'Eglise. Situation actuelle et réflexion théologique," in *Responsabilités internationales des chrétiens* (Ouvr. Coll.) (Paris: Casterman, 1956), pp. 111-44; "Collégialité et mission," in *Lettre aux Communautés* . . . (1964), n. 4, pp. 19-27; "Réflexions sur l'adaptation," in *Cahiers du Cercle S. J.-B.* (May, 1963), pp. 14-21; "L'homme et la liturgie," in *Lettre aux Communautés* . . . (1962), n. 6, pp. 3-7; "Participation à l'Eucharistie et appartenance à l'Eglise," in *Paroisse et Liturgie* 15/8 (1963), pp. 573-83; "Le baptême est-il au seuil de la vie ecclésiale?", *ibid.*, 15/7 (1963), pp. 517-29; "Liturgie et mission," *ibid.*, 1/7 (1962), pp. 417-24; "Les institutions chrétiennes dans une Eglise missionnaire," in *La Revue Nouvelle*, 15/10 (1963), pp. 270-9; "Pour une théologie des rapports entre la mission et la paroisse," *ibid.*, 15/6 (1962), pp. 579-92; "La paroisse, centre d'évangélisation," in *Paroisse et Liturgie* 15/8 (1963), pp. 584-99; "Paroisse rurale et exigences actuelles de la mission," in *Cahiers du Clergé rural* (August-September, 1963), pp. 20-35; "Prêtres et laïcs au service d'une unique mission," in *La Revue Nouvelle* 15/7 (1961), pp. 3-18; "Prêtres, religieux et laïcs dans le monde actuel," in *Evangéliser* 89 (1961), pp. 451-61; "Réflexions sur le laïcat missionnaire," in *Cahiers du Cercle S.J.-B.* (February, 1962), pp. 15-22; "L'assistant technique, les royaumes de la terre et le royaume de Dieu," in *Terre entière*, n. 2 (1963), pp. 60-70; "Les contestations de la mission," in *Lettre aux Communautés* . . . (1960), n. 9, pp. 3-13; "Attention à la vie et évangélisation," in *Paroisse d'aujourd'hui et évangélisation* (Paris, 1965), pp. 13-41.

[130] Quoted by J. Laloux, *op. cit.* above, footnote 7, p. 43.

[131] *Ibid.*, p. 44.

mon objective which has meaning and value for society as a whole." [132] There are in the Church, as Liégé has well shown, three levels of institutions interrelated as one whole in actual living: (1) *the ecclesial institution* as such, structured by the apostolic powers and gathered around a sacramental institution in its essentials; (2) *ecclesiastical institutions* founded by the Church according to the needs and the times in order to express and acculturate the ecclesial institution; (3) *the temporal Christian institutions* which have an objective that is profane in itself, but linked with the Church because organized or supervised by her. In the Church thus institutionalized, certain realities (those of no. 1) are unchangeable, while others (nos. 2 and 3) are more or less contingent.[133]

Culture, the real substance of social life, lived in a given milieu, represents in a specific social context what men "are", what they "do", the "social values" to which they adhere in that sphere. The institutions of the Church are an element of the culture, and the institutionalizing ways of the Church are conditioned by the surrounding culture which contributes in turn to their fashioning.

Mission demands primarily an acculturating presence, an acculturating action. Missionary work presupposes a process of cooperation, accommodation and assimilation.

By the process of cooperation, the missionary Church adopts the aspirations of the non-Christian world in all their legitimate aspects. By accommodation and assimilation, the Church modifies her behavior pattern and invites the non-Christian world to do the same so as to produce a new state of affairs.

Mission depends ultimately on acculturating motivation, the basis of which is spiritual liberty, inviting the Church to respect non-Christian cultures and to adaptability with regard to her own institutions.

Such is the complexity of the missionary program that its real-

---

[132] *Ibid.*, p. 47.

[133] P.-A. Liégé, "La mission contre les institutions chrétiennes," in *Parole et Mission* 15 (October, 1961), pp. 495 ff. On the whole question of acculturation, see the important article, "Mission et culture non-chrétiennes," in *Semaine de Missiologie de Louvain* (Brüges/Paris, 1960).

ization is impossible without the collaboration of the whole Church and even without a certain spiritual unanimity, clearly seen in the Acts of the Apostles. Overly great tensions between Christian groups endanger the coherence of ecclesial action, as the study of Siefer on the priest-workers shows.[134]

Extent of the Mission

One of the points on which discussion has been and continues to be most lively is the question as to whether mission is connected with a territory or attached to any human space.[135]

The theology of *plantatio Ecclesiae*, interpreted in a strictly juridical way as the act of setting up the structures and institutions of the Church, brought out a formal distinction between mission and the work of pastors, defined thereafter as two aspects of one thing: the apostolate. This definition of missions, which does not attach them directly to the mission of the Church, is clearly not *theological*, for it would make them something apart from the Church. In spite of the possibly mistaken fear of numerous missionaries—seeing the revival of the notion of mission as compromising missionary vocations for mission countries—it is absolutely necessary to define mission as a function of missionary situations that are completely dissimilar. The differences are not in the mission, but are entirely in the situation before which, or in which, the Church finds herself, and which causes her to act differently, using activities and methods of her own. One might distinguish the following situations: making a young Church exist where it is not yet truly present; the presence of a young Church which has not yet all the required resources within herself; a Church which is already old, but for various reasons finds herself in difficult circumstances or has remained at too low a level; lastly, a Church fully implanted, perhaps of long standing, but which, besides being obliged to evangelize the world, has within herself undeveloped parts where truly she does not exist for a particular group of men. These may not be territories, except

[134] G. Siefer, *La mission des prêtres-ouvriers* (Paris, 1960), p. 32.
[135] See the résumé of this discussion in E. Loffeld, *op. cit.*, pp. 330-6.

accidentally, but they are men and human areas within a Church which determine the missionary situations in which the unique mission of the Church is enacted.[136]

Missionary theory today must be solidly based on the fundamental hypothesis of achristianization; we find ourselves facing a new world, compared to the Christianity of yesterday, a world which has practically never been evangelized in its new aspects, namely, the whole social, cultural and socio-cultural system.[137]

"Evangelization," Le Guillou wrote, "can no longer be defined by geographical norms, but by human milieux. Essentially, it confronts human problems belonging to a psychology, a culture, historical religions or a climate of dechristianization; it is through and in this environment that conversion must be stirred up and

---

[136] J. Thomas, "Les 'espaces' de la Mission," in *Parole et Mission* 4, pp. 16-33.

[137] See the excellent sociological analysis of J. Laloux, *op. cit.*, pp. 67-8: "It is a fact that never in the past has the Church been confronted with a world that was technological, democratic, opened to planetary space, such as we know it today, with a world that is pluralistic and profane as we see at present and in which the Church is a minority. Inasmuch as this world has not been evangelized in the course of its formation, it is utopian to believe that it was to remain and could remain Christian simply because it followed in time upon a world that had been Christian in its own way (that is, in a totally different context); and it is erroneous and to a certain extent unjust to say that it had been dechristianized when, in fact, it had gradually abandoned a type of Christianity which—rightly or wrongly is not the point—had less and less meaning in the eyes of many people. And what can be said of the children born afterwards in these milieux where unbelief, or at least the absence of religion, had become the norm for familial and social behavior?

"Certainly, we repeat, 'dechristianization' and 'achristianization' are closely allied phenomena. But whatever may have been the case in the past and whatever be the process which evolved to bring about the present situation, it is essential to realize that the fundamental situation today is that the modern world is achristian because it has not been evangelized. Such a viewpoint really affects the idea and execution of missionary plans, because it is not a matter of indifference whether we think that a person has abandoned a thing or that he has never had it, when our concern is with giving it to him." See also the valuable note on the achristianization of today's world, pp. 183-96, where J. Laloux shows clearly the profound changes: "This way of life and these values, partially or totally new, have given modern man a new ambition for inserting his own person into society, and this necessitates a distinctly new frame of reference with regard to all civil or religious authority and with regard to God" (p. 290).

faith brought to life. It is involved in the great human spiritual currents that flow through all humanity in our day.

"The mission of the Church must be contemplated as a whole before speaking of the ecclesial missionary groups which must be more and more capable of constant change in order to adapt to the changing reality that is to be evangelized. It is quite clear, for example, that a static and institutional view of mission keeps us from the necessary realization that the Western world, like all the rest, is a world in need of evangelization. Only a view of the dynamic reality of the mystery of Christ can give us a hold on a world that is rapidly evolving in the process of working out its own culture.

"Mission is often in crisis because it is still too closely linked by many with a geographic vision or a perspective of Christendom, instead of taking its full anthropological dimension by which it is united to the entire destiny of the human race.

"At a time when the historicity of man is thought of more and more in terms of universal history, at a time when not only his individual destiny but, very specifically, that of the whole human race preoccupies contemporary man, at a time when humanity takes on the shape of a spiritual reality conscious of its solidarity, it would be disastrous for mission not to reveal itself in all its world-wideness and in all its unity in a revalidating of specifically missionary vocations." [138]

It should be noted, moreover, that a favorable condition for mission stems from the fact that the Church in Vatican Council II has recovered the combination of values whose deficiency greatly impeded her development: the meaning of pluralism, collegiality, the laity, a more mystical and dynamic vision of the Church.[139]

Conclusion

In tracing, however partially, the stages in the restoration of mission in ecclesiology, one is struck by the enormous field of

[138] G. Mercier and M.-J. Le Guillou, *op. cit.* above, footnote 74.
[139] For a criticism of the mission in its history see the book quoted on the preceding page.

labor that has opened up in the past thirty years and by the vitality of the movement behind this activity. The movement seems like a prehistory of the Council.

John XXIII had perceived this when he directed the Council toward reflection by the Church on her own life, in the face of Christian pluralism and before the world. This meant making mission the integrating principle of all ecclesial action and emphasizing that, since mission is an analogous concept, it will come to be recognized by all Christians as the life of the Spirit and the norm of their actions. This led to the revelation of the future requirements for the Church's vitality.

At first an ecclesiological fact, mission (coextensive with the manifestation of the Spirit) becomes more and more clearly an ecclesiological theme.

More distinctly today than originally, in days of full vitality, mission is seen as the common action of all the holy People of God, an action belonging equally to the bishop and to Christians, to the priestly ministry and to contemplative grace, but only inasmuch as it elicits individual commitment: the sociological and charismatic quality that a pluralistic world requires. Ecclesiology is a help to this missionary attitude.

More distinctly, also, the touchstone of mission and catholicity is seen to be the conversion brought about by encountering the poor, simply and on all levels of the life of the Church. Ecclesiology sheds light on this without hiding anything.

This rediscovery of mission has been done haltingly. It is still represented today by many ideas that are not yet completely settled in their relations with one another and still to be investigated theologically. The reflections and discussions that we have suggested need to be reviewed at leisure, sifted and rethought. Certainly, starting with mission—as an ecclesiological concept and as a special ecclesial experience—in the theological vision of mystery, the whole of ecclesiology in its unity can be revised in view of the mission that is so urgent in this era.

PART III

DOCUMENTATION
CONCILIUM

Office of the Executive Secretary
Nijmegen, Netherlands

Hans Heimerl/*Graz, Austria*

The Concept of Laity
in the Constitution
on the Church

A cursory reading of the *Constitution on the Church* of Vatican Council II shows that it does not employ a uniform notion of "laity". The eventual publication of the complete Council proceedings and the intervening lapse of time will allow definitive commentaries to appear.[1] Meanwhile, this article is a preliminary attempt to indicate the various aspects and tendencies that make up the occasionally differing concepts of laity in the conciliar text.

I

THE ANALOGOUS CONCEPT OF LAITY

A main concern of the Council was to express its prescriptions about the laity in new formulas, although obviously on the basis of prevailing conceptions and ideas. To understand the Constitution correctly, one must acquaint himself with the current notions of laity that were also brought forward or presupposed during the second session in the discussion on the chapter on the laity.

[1] F. Wulf, "Fragen um den Christen in der Welf," in *Geist und Leben* 38 (1965), pp. 300-9 and B. Dreher, "Würde und Sendung des Laien," in *Lebendige Seelsorge* 16 (1965), pp. 214-20 are discussions which take as their point of departure the chapter on the laity rather than actual commentaries.

Determined by differing historical situations as well as by varying
theological approaches, the notions of laity occupy a whole range
of meaning that precludes any narrow classification.

Every ecclesial definition of the laity begins with a generic
element. The enthusiasm with which the higher evaluation of the
lay state has been greeted gives the impression that the layman
is wholly distinct from the clergy and religious, that he has primarily only his proper task to fulfill and his peculiar rights to
defend. Actually, this is not so. For every Christian, lay or
clerical, one, universal, essential status determines his very existence as a Christian in all its ramifications.[2] Most features of
Christian existence and activity are precisely the same for priests
and laity. The generic element is something positive and is common to all concepts of laity, though not always duly appreciated
as such.

Whenever the word "laity" is used without understanding this
basic generic element, it is no longer possible to speak of an
ecclesial concept of laity, nor even of an analogous concept, but
only of an equivocal one. Whenever one speaks about the "lay
character" (*laicità*) of the State or even about laicism, this has
really nothing to do with the ecclesial notion of laity. The final
text of the *Constitution on the Church*, as distinguished from the
original proposals, does not employ the word in this sense and it
appears as such only in a footnote citing Pius XII.[3]

The specific element that distinguishes the lay state from others
in the Church plays a subordinate role when this element is seen
in the light of what it means to be a Christian. But this specific
difference virtually changes in the various definitions of laity. If
we may be allowed to generalize for the sake of giving a survey
of these definitions, we can list the following:

1. *Negative, Single-Pole Concept*

The layman is regarded or even defined as one who is not a
cleric. This negative definition is usually bound up with the idea

[2] Cf. F. Klostermann, *Das christliche Apostolat* (Innsbruck, 1962), pp.
765ff.

[3] Note 116: "Laicità dello Stato."

of the passivity of the laity expressed in the slogan "the listening and learning Church" and is found cropping up in present-day catechisms even during conciliar debates. The qualification "single-pole" shows that there is but one point of reference from which the distinction is made, namely, that of the cleric.

2. *Negative, Double-Pole Concept*

In this view, the layman is neither a cleric nor a religious; he therefore exhibits neither their qualifications nor their "prerogatives". Like the first definition, this can be understood best in the light of medieval society in which clerics and monks closely resembled one another in their manner of living and privileges, and were, in their "ecclesiastical" status, contrasted to the laity, who were represented by worldly powers. The classical expression of this view of the laity is the often cited passage from the *Decree of Gratian*: "There are two types of Christians: one is consecrated to divine service, contemplation and prayer . . . these are the clerics and the members of the orders. . . . But there is also another type of Christian, the layman . . . who is allowed to marry, to cultivate the earth. . . ." [4]

3. *Positive, Essential Concept*

The layman enjoys all the values and has all the duties of being a Christian; he shares the generic element of what it means to be a Christian, but he has a positive and active role also, inasmuch as he differs from the cleric. The layman's relation to the hierarchy is not only that of a certain separation but, above all, of an exchange promoting the activity of both parties. In his own way, the layman participates in the communal worship of the Church, cooperates personally in the reception of the sacraments and, under the leadership and direction of the hierarchy, contributes to the edification of the body of Christ. This concept deserves to be called "essential" because it approaches most closely the theological essence of the layman. It is "single-pole" because it is based upon a single principle of distinction, namely, the relation of exchange between clergy and laity.

[4] Cf. c. 7, C XII, q. 1.

4. *Positive, Existential Concept*

The essence of the layman does not fulfill itself in a vacuum, but is accompanied by a number of accidental elements that determine the layman in his concrete existence. For example, the hierarchical authority of the cleric limits him primarily to the exercise of this authority so that the fashioning of the world is "left" to the layman (cf. 31b).[5] But if we now direct our attention beyond this essential aspect to what the layman ordinarily is and what he does concretely from an empirical, sociological viewpoint, we come to the existential concept that defines him particularly in relation to his place in the world and his task for the world. Actually, most laymen exercise a profession in the world and (in contrast to the Western clergy) within married life: as a general rule, they stand in the world. We leave aside the question whether many contemporary authors are justified in constructing a definition of laity from this premise, thus making essential what is actually existential. In any case, this concept of laity is "double-pole" inasmuch as it distinguishes the concrete, world-oriented layman from both clerics and religious.

II

THE CHAPTER ON THE LAITY

Chapter IV of the *Constitution on the Church* (31a) contains a *determination of the concept* of laity: "The term laity is here understood to mean all the faithful except those in holy orders and those in the state of religious life especially approved by the Church. These faithful are by baptism made one body with Christ and are constituted the People of God; they are in their own way made sharers in the priestly, prophetical and kingly functions of Christ, and they carry out for their own part the mission of the whole Christian people in the Church and in the world."

[5] References to the *Constitution on the Church* are made throughout this article according to the number of the section in the text, while individual paragraphs within each section are indicated by lowercase letters.

The form of this statement indicates that the Council did not intend to give a definition (though such was often proposed in the conciliar debates), but merely a determination of limited scope, almost a simple rule of grammar similar to the legal definitions in the Code of Canon Law that are not maintained consistently. When we ask to what extent the Council intends that this rule of grammar bind (What is the meaning of "is *here* understood"?), we find it narrow indeed. Two chapters further on (43b), we read that the religious state of life is not an intermediary state between the clerical and lay states but rather a state of life made up of members of both states. Chapter IV distinguishes the lay state from both the clerical and the religious states, while Chapter VI, like canon 107 of the Code of Canon Law, allows religious to also be laity. The chapter on the laity uses a double-pole concept, while that on religious prefers a single-pole concept. Thus, the various determinations of the concept are limited specifically to the respective chapters in which they appear and, as we shall see, these determinations may vary in shading even within one and the same chapter.

The explication of the term laity in Chapter IV has two parts. The first represents a negative, double-pole concept, whereas the second ("These faithful. . . .") clarifies the former by describing the *generic* element of the lay state. The phrases "in their own way" and "for their own part" merely hint at the special manner of being a Christian proper to the layman. This paragraph, containing the actual limitation of the concept of laity, does not refer to a *specific, positive* element proper to the lay state. Only in the following paragraph do we encounter a carefully worded reference to this specific element: "What specifically characterizes the laity is their *secular nature*."

The expressions further describing the peculiarities of the lay state come down to a list of approximations. Clerics are not set apart entirely from the things of this world but may be "at times engaged in secular activities" and are *"especially* and professedly ordained to the sacred ministry". The laity, on the other hand, live in the *"ordinary"* circumstances of family and social life

(How do we distinguish these from "extraordinary" circumstances?) and it is their *special* (not exclusive) vocation to order
all temporal realities through Christ to the Father (31b). The
witness of the laity in life and word has a *specific* quality in that
it is carried out in the *ordinary* surroundings of the world (35b).

If we take section 31 as a whole, it is evident from its conscious restriction to a nominal definition and from its vague description of the element specific to the laity that the Council had
no intention of defining, expressly or even in passing, the essence
of the lay state or even of making a clear statement about it.
Within the confines of this section of the chapter on the laity, the
Council takes as its axis of reference the existential concept of
laity without however conferring any generally binding force
upon this point of view.

The *remaining sections* of Chapter IV refer frequently to the
world as the area in which the laity accomplish their vocation.
These references are not simply indicative but rather *imperative,*
in form (35a ending, 36c, 38) or at least in intention (33a:
"They are called upon. . . ."; 35a, 35d, 36b).

Two places in the chapter on the laity and one in the chapter
on the universal vocation to holiness mention laymen who enter
into closer relation with the hierarchy, participate in the apostolic
mission of the Church (33b) or even perform religious duties
(*officia sacra*) in place of sacred ministers (35d) and thus nearly
come to be counted among the clergy (41d). According to many
champions of the existential concept of laity, a layman who functions in the service of the Church is not really a layman since he
is no longer distinguished by his standing in the world but shares
in the hierarchical powers.[6] The text of the Constitution uses the
word "layman" for such a person without going into the theoretical problem involved in this designation.

We notice rearing its head here and there in the chapter on the
laity a tendency surely not in accord either with the intention of
the majority of the Council fathers or with the basic tone of the

[6] K. Rahner, Schriften zur Theologie II (Einsiedeln, [5]1961), pp. 340ff.
and 344 (Eng. tr.: *Theological Investigations* II [Baltimore: Helicon,
1964]).

chapter itself. I call this the *"outsider-current"* because it looks upon the layman as an outsider in the Church. Church means the clergy and religious; the laity do not belong "properly" but only additionally or "also". This unfortunate viewpoint appears to be represented in the repeated *"also* the laity" (34a, 34b, 35a, 36a, 33d), although the intention was to say the exact opposite: the laity as well as the clergy or religious have such and such duties or rights. Section 33 speaks of the laity as having the capacity of assuming from the hierarchy certain *ecclesiastical* functions. This looks as if "ecclesiastical" means the same as "not really for the laity". It is true that *munera ecclesiastica* is a term consecrated by the Code of Canon Law;[7] yet, the very fact that the Council feels itself bound to this terminology indicates the extent to which the embers of the old "outsider-current" still glow beneath the ashes. Most striking of all is the reversal suffered by the teaching of the chapter on the People of God concerning the *universal* priesthood (10; cf. 26c and 28) when this comes up again in the paragraph on the "spiritual" priesthood of the laity (34b). The real *exercise* of a universal priesthood through co-operation in the eucharistic celebration and the reception of the sacraments, as clearly set out in the earlier chapter, deteriorates into the spiritual offering made (passively) in the eucharist.

Of far greater importance, however, are the statements regarding the *active cooperation* and *mutual exchanges* between hierarchy and laity: the hierarchy is not set up to take upon itself the entire salvific mission of the Church; its role is rather to "shepherd the faithful . . . so that all according to their proper roles may cooperate in this common undertaking with one mind" (30). "For the distinction that the Lord made between sacred ministers and the rest of the People of God bears within it a certain union, since pastors and the other faithful are bound to each other by a mutual necessity. Pastors of the Church, following the example of the Lord, should minister to one another and to the faithful. These in their turn should enthusiastically lend their joint assistance to their pastors and teachers. Thus, in their

[7] Cf. Can. 145, § 1.

diversity all bear witness to the wonderful unity in the body of Christ" (32c). In section 37a-c we find some indication of the spirit and mode of operation that is to characterize this cooperative effort. This idea of fruitful exchange is the ground upon which rests the essential concept of laity that even the Council seems to recognize as being at least the underpinning of an existential concept.

The *generic element* of the concept of laity, representing the vocation and the dignity common to all Christians, is particularly stressed in articles 32b-33a. Baptism and consequent membership in the Church are the basis of this universal quality (32b, 33a-b). This common base takes precedence over the role peculiar to the laity even where it is a matter of their participation in the priesthood and in the prophetic and witnessing office as well as in the kingship of Christ. This is actually the positive significance of the poorly worded phrase "also the laity".

If we consider the chapter as a whole, we are struck by the *various levels* of meaning found in the concept of laity used here and must agree with Ratzinger's complaint that a truly positive definition of laity is not to be found in view of the excessive dependence of the present definition upon factors that are secular rather than ecclesial.[8] Yet, two facts soften the impact of this criticism: (1) the emphasis upon the generic element and upon the active exchange between hierarchy and laity, and (2) the need of understanding the chapter on the laity in the light of the aims of both the entire Council and of this particular chapter. Vatican Council II aimed at being an essentially pastoral Council. One of the Council fathers, introducing his contribution to a conciliar debate, said: *"Theologi non sumus, sed pastores tantum."*

The Council wanted to appeal to and encourage the layman as he works within the present-day Church and her lay movements and to educate the pastors toward an up-to-date attitude concerning their flocks. Exactness of formulation and attempts at systematization were subordinated to this primary intention, even if

---

[8] J. Ratzinger, *Das Konzil auf dem Weg. Rückblick auf die zweite Sitzungsperiode* (Cologne, 1965), pp. 42f.

something was lost in the process. The Council did not ask itself what a layman is, but rather what is the mission proper to the numerically largest group in the Church today. It is *not* a question of *definition*. It is a question of *pastoral instruction*, for which a nominal description in approximate terms suffices.

III

LAITY IN THE REMAINING CHAPTERS

No more than in reference to the Code of Canon Law may one say that the *Constitution on the Church* treats the subject of the laity only in that section headed *"De laicis"*. The chapter on the laity refers back to all that was said about the People of God as being valid for the laity as well as for clerics and religious. In fact, the *Constitution on the Church* has a great deal more to say about the laity than even this.

The chapter on the hierarchical structure of the Church refers to bishops and priests in terms that could suggest passivity on the part of the laity: *regere, gubernare, pascere, docere* and *sanctificare*. But in this, and particularly in other chapters, there are indications of the active role played by the laity in the exchange mentioned above. Besides, it would be impossible to include everything in every single passage. This Constitution repeats itself enough as it is (the vocation of married couples: 11b, 35c, 41e; frequent stress upon primacy, etc.), so that it would be tiring to find the active role of the laity on behalf of the hierarchy underlined in every possible connection.

Various parts of the Constitution offer an approach toward a *positive evaluation* of the laity that occasionally exceeds the intrinsic merit of the chapter on the laity itself. There are notably three assertions that keep coming up in various contexts:

1. *The Fullness of Christian Dignity and Mission*

This theme treats the "original status" of the Christian—the generic element in the concept of laity—as the treasure of Christian existence rather than as a narrow basis of unity among the three states in the Church. The very first chapter—on the mystery of the Church—refers to each of the faithful as a temple of the Holy Spirit (4a) and as one into whom is poured the life of Christ to whom each is united through baptism (7b). The chapter on the People of God may be called rightly the theological foundation for the chapter on the laity.[9] Though rarely calling him by name, it describes the layman in his capacity as member of the People of God. He belongs to "a chosen race, a royal priesthood, a holy nation" (9a, citing 1 Pet. 2, 9f.). This is why he enjoys a universal priesthood, exercised in the personal offering of spiritual cult and in a life of virtue as well as in his participation in the eucharistic sacrifice and in the active reception of the sacraments (10-11). These assertions far surpass in extent and in theological profundity the parallel statements found in the chapter on the laity. On the other hand, the sharing of all the faithful in the prophetic office of Christ is handled very briefly, primarily in the context of the sense of faith and the infallibility of the People of God *in credendo*. The chapter on the universal vocation to holiness takes to task, indirectly, the opinions that holiness is a matter for priests and religious only and that there exists an entirely special spirituality for laymen. It insists again and again that all the faithful of all states are called to the fullness of Christian life and perfect love (39, 40b, 41a, 41g, 42e).

2. *The Diversity of Spiritual Gifts*

The diversity of spiritual gifts determines both the distinction between the members of the mystical body, the People of God, and the differences in their respective duties and services (7c, 7e, 12b). Among these charisms, one must not understand merely the extraordinary graces but ought to include the more usual and matter-of-fact gifts (12b). The grace of apostleship is only one of these spiritual gifts and the hierarchical gifts hardly exhaust the charismatic graces. The Constitution does not expressly say, but does intimate, that the secular vocation is not simply a separate calling (31b), but also a special gift of grace. Every Christian must increase daily in holiness according to his

[9] J. Ratzinger in the Introduction to the German edition of the *Constitution on the Church* (Munich, 1965); *Herder Korr.* 19 (1964/65), p. 162.

own gifts and graces (*secundum propria dona et munera*), and examples are cited of married couples and parents, of those engaged in heavy labor and of the poor and infirm (41e, 41f). One would even suspect that to be a layman in the sense of engaging in active exchange with the hierarchy is a specific grace.

3. *The Active Exchange between Clergy and Laity*

Using their gifts of grace, the members of the Church do not only act from the higher to the lower level, but are *mutually* helpful to one another (7e). Universal priesthood and official priesthood are *ordered to one another* since both share in a special way in the priesthood of Christ (10b). In every liturgical service, each of the faithful acts his proper part, not indiscriminately, but each in his own way (11a; cf. 26a and 62b). The sense of faith is an answer in reply to the sacred teaching office of the Church (12a; cf. 25a). Every disciple of Christ has the obligation of spreading the faith according to his state (17). The ministers in the Church serve their brethren so that all who are of the People of God may work toward a common goal and arrive at salvation (18a). To this end, the bishops must arouse the ardent cooperation of the faithful (23c, 27c; cf. 65).

IV

INFERENCES FOR EXPLICATION AND APPLICATION OF THE CONSTITUTION

The existential concept of the laity found in Chapter IV has to be understood in light of the *restrictions* set by the Council itself and of its *pastoral execution*. This is the only way to avoid the *danger of misinterpretation* in attempts to transfer this concept into systematic theology. The existential, double-pole concept that singles out the secular commitment as the specific note of the layman is not intended to be a definition of his essence and ought not to be put forth as such. Otherwise, the unfortunate development that took place in the theory of Catholic Action may find its counterpart here. At that time, some commentators tried to bring the practical and pastoral instructions of Pius XI, limited as they were by the situation in which they arose, into scholastic categories, thereby arriving at a valueless exegesis of the expressions "mandate", "participation in the hierarchical apostolate", etc. Above all, it is a question of acting in line with the spirit of the chapter on the laity, and only secondarily can this spirit indicate an orientation for the theological problem on the essence of laity. The formulas used can serve as checkpoints only when seen in the light of the spirit of the chapter.

In the area of practical implementation, the existential concept is dangerously open to *misapplication*. When the layman is assigned the world as his special field of operation, it can easily happen that religion becomes important only for the clergy, and this can result finally in a confirmation of the already noticeable tendency to deny to the hierarchy any influence in shaping the world. On the other hand, the layman would no longer feel that he "belongs" in the Church and the "outsider-current" would gain ground. In this way, the very heart would be cut out of the chapter on the laity, namely, the stress upon the layman's full, active membership in the Church.

Even more than protection from the dangers of misinterpretation and misapplication, the concept of laity found in Chapter IV needs completion from a *deeper and fuller understanding of what the layman really is*. A first step in this direction was taken by the Council itself in the *Constitution on the Church,* especially in the chapter on the People of God. The *Decree on the Apostolate of the Laity* and the *Constitution on the Church in the Modern World* offer new points of view. The ecumenical dialogue will show that the separated Christians often have different conceptions of the laity. The future development in the Catholic Church and in secular society will overtake the situation from which the present chapter on the laity was written. In this way, a growth in the concept of laity will take place that will lead, on the one hand, to a deeper appreciation of essentials, and, on the other, to progress in practical implementation.

Some Observations on the Article by Hans Heimerl

This small study of the concept of laity and its various meanings in the *Constitution on the Church* seems to me worthwhile because it shows that a casual treatment of terminology can have important practical results. In itself terminology may be very innocuous, but very often it determines the way in which our attention is led to practical considerations. Yet, there seem to be a few things in this study that are somewhat overemphasized. It is true that Chapters IV and VI do not use the notion of "laity" in exactly the same way. But Chapter VI (*De Religiosis*) sought above all to avoid a teaching of three classes and to stress that the division into clergy and laity must not be confused with the distinction between religious and non-religious, a confusion that would lead to these "three classes" in the Church. And so, since there was no carefully distinguished terminology, which even a Council cannot create out of the blue, one can understand that the text used the terminology of the Code of Canon Law. The real notion of "laity" is described in Chapter IV. It obviously contains all that was said about the "People of God" in Chapter II, and did not need repetition.

Heimerl's distinction between a "positive essential concept" and a "positive existential concept" is not altogether clear to me. If the layman, in spite of his membership in the People of God which he shares with clergy and religious together with all the rights and duties this implies, is nevertheless distinguished from the clergy and religious, then his special relation to the world must be part of his "essential concept" unless we want to distinguish him in a purely negative way from the clergy and religious. Therefore, it seems to me that, in point of fact, the "essential" and "existential" cannot be distinguished, particularly the active application to the clergy in whose official function there is still something that applies to all members of the People of God, and therefore also to the clergy (vis-à-vis a higher functionary) and religious; and so, this does not by itself distinguish laymen from clergy and religious. When Heimerl detects an undertone of "outsider" in the expression "also the laity", he seems to exaggerate. Given the present terminology and the still existing clerical mentality, the Council could only emphasize that whatever was said about all the members of the People of God *obviously* "also" referred to the laity. Heimerl grants that the Council was opposed to this treatment of the layman as an "outsider". But since it happens to exist, it was really impossible to put it in another way.

Lastly, it seems to me that one should not exaggerate the distinction between a pastoral and a dogmatic statement.

KARL RAHNER, S.J.

————◆◀◈▶◆————

Heimerl's contribution to the examination of the concept of "laity" deserves much credit because of its clarity and the prudence of its nuances. For the non-Catholic the key to any interpretation of the laity is and remains the connection of the required professional qualifications and clerical ordination on the one hand with the unavoidable lack of expertise, secularity and passivity on the other.

Why has this only recently become a Church problem? The answer seems to me to lie in the fact that only recently has the layman become recognized as an articulate, responsible and capable man in religious matters (the image of the shepherd and the sheep of the flock is no longer acceptable); secondly, because at the same time far more frequent appeal is made to his collaboration in a great variety of problems, not only in matters of administration and organization, but also in spiritual and religious affairs such as education, youth work and sometimes even preaching and pastoral care, whence the introduction or renewal of the diaconate. Thus it appears that such lay work can be of high quality. A third aspect in this development is the scarcity of clergy in both the Catholic and Protestant Churches, so that it also appears as if only this need drove the Churches to an awareness of the possibilities and opportunities of assistance in this field. A lay *apostolate* always presupposes more professional knowledge, dedication, active mastery and cultivation of the spiritual life than is altogether identifiable with the word "lay".

The change in linguistic use makes the layman a *non-expert,* possibly an amateur, but this meaning pays no attention to ordination or to religious implications.

On the Protestant side, in a different ecclesial context, it is much more widely recognized that the so-called universal priesthood of the faithful is really a fiction, or rather, more a requirement than a reality. There are only a few sects where there are no ecclesiastical offices. In the larger denominations, even where the right to preach is exceptionally linked with "special gifts", practically all activity in the congregation is entrusted to the minister, elder or deacon. In emergencies (*Dieu a besoin des hommes*) a layman without ordination is sometimes called upon, but that is not the rule. On the other hand, the Protestant world, too, recognizes new services along with the old offices.

The nature of the work done in such a ministry does not require a specifically *theological* expertise, and so religious training through religious instruction and confession may be enough, but this does not mean that such members of the community can be "lay" in the field entrusted to them, whether it is the Sunday school, or women's work, or the formation of a group of workingmen, or a "sub"-community at a university. This corresponds to what Heimerl calls the "positive" side of being a layman in his article. There the clergyman is a layman. He may pronounce a word of consecration or say Mass, but his authority does not extend beyond his proficiency.

Behind this new active lay work there also lies, of course, a rather important change in the structure and nature of the congregation and the Church, a change stretching deep down into the religious life. This is the growing sense of mission in a world that is losing its civilized quality, the growing need to give meaning to a daily existence dominated by job and leisure.

When, therefore, people ask for a theology of the layman, they really mean a theology of the—mainly social—services, and for a new formulation of the militant Church in what is called a post-Christian world: in other words, an elaboration of Schema XIII!

People who would find this a too hurried and exaggerated secularization have, in my opinion, not yet understood the present situation of Christendom. Moreover, they underrate the extent and depth of the *biblical* formation required for this lay work. The point of reference for this lay work in Church and congregation lies in the knowledge of the Bible and the constant living companionship with Holy Scripture. This does not mean, of course, that for many of these tasks one can lightheartedly dispense with a deeper philosophical knowledge of Church and world. But then, of course, the layman becomes more than a layman. Finally, the religious and theological perspective of such an active Christian life is found in a constantly deeper penetration and putting into practice of the work of Christ, the servant. For such a sacramental-minded Church as Roman Catholicism, this might well suggest a restoration of the "washing of the feet" (John 13) to the place of honor which this shabbily treated action deserves in the Church of Christ.   LAMBERTUS VAN HOLK

Only to a limited extent is the theology of the lay state determined by abstract, universally valid principles. Rather than an analysis and ordering of abstract concepts, it is theological reflection upon the concrete institutional structure of the Church, a structure which, while always keeping some features the same, is historically conditioned and subject to change. It is, then, a fallacy to suppose that to find a definition of the unchanging essence of the lay state is adequately to determine the role of the layman in the concrete. The present shift in the layman's position in the Church and the spate of discussion about it are simply part of a general transition affecting the whole structure of the Church. The Church is gradually shedding an historical embodiment which has endured for centuries and is feeling her way toward a new sociological structure appropriate to her situation in the modern world. The real problem is to work out ecclesial structures and functions in the concrete, and here universal, non-historical principles and definitions can be only a partial guide.

If the problem of the layman's state and function is taken in isolation, it is incapable of complete solution. The papacy, the episcopate and the presbyterate as well as the lay state are historically conditioned in their social structure, in the precise determination of their functions and in the manner in which these are exercised. As a social body with an institutional structure, the Church never exists as a pure essence stripped of incidental, transitory features. What exists is a particular historical realization of that essence. The same applies to all her institutional offices and functions. The problem today is as much a problem of determining the precise structure and function of the Church's ordained ministry as a problem of marking out the role of the layman. One and the same problem is in question, namely, the adaptation of the entire institutional setup of the Church to a new situation.

To talk, therefore, simply of a new understanding of the lay state is to miss the fact that a radical rethinking of all the social structures of the Church is necessary. Certainly, the way has been prepared for this by a new emphasis on what all Christians have in common, irrespective of their particular function in the Church, and by a new recognition of the indispensable part played by the layman in the mission of the Church to the world. But if these truths are to be embodied in the structure of the Church, the profound changes required will have to extend to the clergy as well as the laity.

As a matter of fact, much less in the institutional structure of the Church comes from divine law and much more from passing historical and social causes than is generally acknowledged. But this is obscured by the habit of thinking of the Church at one remove from reality. The doctrine of the papacy or the episcopate or the presbyterate does not suffice to tell us how these offices exist and function in the concrete. Empirical sociological studies, supplemented by corresponding historical investigations—for example, of the structure of power within the Church, of the various patterns of decision-making, of the modalities in the exercise of episcopal authority, of the varying social relationship between priest and people—would give a new dimension to our knowledge of the Church as an institution. At this level the social structure of the Church is subject to change. The relation between bishop and priest or between priest and layman, the pattern of decision-making, the distribution of responsibility, and so on, can be very different sociologically without any difference in doctrinal principle being involved. But it is at this concrete level that it will be decided whether the high doctrine of the lay state remains a beautiful ideal or is made effectual in practice.

In brief, the theology of the lay state should not confine itself to the universal and unchanging, devoting itself as in the past almost exclusively to constructing a universally valid concept of the layman and his role. It should become reflection upon the social structure of the Church in all its empirical, concrete, historically conditioned reality. With the aid of the auxiliary sciences of constitutional law and sociology, it should study and promote the institutional changes necessary for the adaptation of the entire social structure of the Church to its situation in modern society. The new structure, like all past embodiments of the Church's reality, will be relative. An absolute ideal structure is a non-historical abstraction.

CHARLES DAVIS

BIOGRAPHICAL NOTES

EUGENE HILLMAN, C.S.SP.: Born November 2, 1924, in Boston, Mass. He joined the Holy Ghost Fathers and was ordained in 1950. He pursued his studies at his order's seminary in Norwalk, Conn., earning a degree in theology. For a year he taught Church history in the Major Seminary of the Moshi diocese of Tanzania. In 1952 he was the first priest ever to be sent to do missionary work among the nomadic tribes of northern Tanzania. Among his published works is *The Church and Mission*. He has contributed articles on the theory of missionary practice to *The African Ecclesiastical Review, The Clergy Review, Homiletic and Pastoral Review* and *The Catholic World*.

KARL MÜLLER, S.V.D.: Born in Blankenberg, Germany. He joined the Society of the Divine Word and was ordained in 1948. He pursued his studies at the Gregorian University in Rome, earning a doctorate in missiology in 1952, and at the University of Münster, earning a doctorate in theology in 1961. He taught Church history and missiology in Siegburg from 1952 until he was appointed Rector of St. Pius College in Münster in 1960. In 1962 he was transferred to Rome, where he is now Prefect of Studies at his order's House of Studies. Among his published works are *Missionsstudien* (1962) and *Die Weltmission der Kirche* (1963).

WALBERT BÜHLMANN, O.F.M.CAP.: Born August 6, 1916, in Lucerne, Switzerland. He became a Capuchin and was ordained in 1942. He pursued his studies at the University of Fribourg where he earned a doctorate in theology. From 1950 to 1953 he did missionary work in Dar es Salaam. Since 1954 he has directed the Institute of Missionary Studies in Fribourg, and has undertaken a number of fact-finding studies during extensive visits to India, Indonesia and various African countries. Among his published works are *Afrika, gestern, heute, morgen* (1960), *Der ewige Auftrag in der Heutigen Zeit* (1961), *Die Kirche unter den Völkern* (1963) and *Pionier der Einheit. Bischof A. Hartmann* (1966). He is an active contributor to missionary reviews.

MARK FANG CHE-YONG, S.J.: Born November 26, 1926, in China. He became a Jesuit and was ordained in 1955. He pursued his studies at the Propaganda Fide University in Rome, the Pontifical Biblical Institute in Munich, and at Comillas University in Spain. He is at present professor of Sacred Scripture and instructor in Hebrew in the Theological Faculty in

Baguio, Philippines. His published works include *Erde, die Ihn trug* (1962) on aspects of the life of Christ, and *Pars theseos: Quaestiones theologicae selectae libri Sira* (1963), which is a study of theological problems arising from the Book of Sirach. He is also a contributor to theological reviews.

MARIE-JOSEPH LE GUILLOU, O.P.: Born December 25, 1920, in Servel (Côtes-du-Nord), France. He became a Dominican and was ordained in 1947. He pursued his studies at the Sorbonne in Paris, at Le Saulchoir, Etiolles, France, and at the University of Athens, earning his doctorate in theology in 1959. He is a member of the Centre d'Etudes Istina, professor of Oriental theology and missiology at Le Saulchoir, and director of the school of ecumenical research at the Catholic Institute in Paris. Among his published works are *L'Esprit de l'Orthodoxie grecque et russe* (1961), *Le Christ et l'Eglise-Théologie du Mystère* (1963), and *Mission et Pauvreté-l'heure de la Mission Mondiale* (1964). He is now preparing a study on the theology of the Holy Spirit, in addition to making regular contributions to theological reviews.

HANS HEIMERL: Born February 15, 1925, in Vienna. He was ordained in 1950 and continued his studies at Graz University and at the Gregorian University, earning doctorates in theology and in canon law. After engaging in pastoral work, he became secretary to the Bishop of Graz, and then professor of canon law in the Theological Faculty of Graz University. Among his published works are *Laien im Dienste der Verkündigung* (1958) and *Kirche, Kierus und Laien-Unterscheidungen und Beziehungen* (1961). Two books on canon law are now in preparation, one studying its theological foundations, the other treating of canon law after the Council.

KARL RAHNER, S.J.: Born March 5, 1904, in Freiburg-im-Breisgau, Germany, he became a Jesuit in 1922. He studied philosophy at Pullach, Germany, taught at Feldkirch, Austria, studied theology at Valenburg, Netherlands, and was ordained in 1932. In 1937 he became a lecturer in Innsbruck, Vienna and Pullach, and in 1948 professor of dogmatic theology at the Leopold-Franzens University in Innsbruck. After numerous theological writings (in which is expressed his central idea: an anthropocentric conception of the whole of theology), Rahner has come to be recognized as one of the most important theological thinkers of the German-speaking world. At present he is professor of Christian thought at the University of Munich.

LAMBERTUS VAN HOLK was an observer at Vatican Council II for the international association of liberal Christianity.

CHARLES DAVIS, a member of the Editorial Board of Concilium, is professor of dogmatic theology at the Pontifical Athenaeum of Philosophy and Theology at Heythrop College, Oxon, England.